Learning to Teach Teaching to Learn

A Holistic Approach

C. DOUG BRYAN

BROADMAN
& HOLMAN
PUBLISHERS

Nashville, Tennessee

Dewey Decimal Classification: 268
Subject Heading: RELIGIOUS EDUCATION
Library of Congress Catalog Number: 92-41814
Printed in the United States of America
Library of Congress Cataloging-in-Publication Data

Bryan, C. Doug, 1954-
  Learning to teach/teaching to learn: a passport to the world
of Christian teaching/learning / C. Doug Bryan.
      p.   cm.
  ISBN 0-8054-6047-0
  1. Christian education—Teaching methods   I. Title.
  BV1534.B75   1993
  268′.6—dc20   92-41814
                                                                  CIP

CONTENTS

This book is dedicated to
two men and two churches—

Kenneth W. Hughey, pastor and friend (deceased)

Donald D. Williford, pastor and friend

Rice Memorial Baptist Church. Greenwood, South Carolina, where I first learned as a teenager

First Baptist Church, Brownwood, Texas, where I teach as an adult

Ministries and friendships shared are long remembered and are long nurturing.

Preface

Learning to Teach/Teaching to Learn is a guide to help readers explore the rewarding yet challenging world of teaching within the Christian church. Christian learning and teaching are intertwined, each influencing and guiding the other. Our Christian heritage involves thousands of years of teaching and learning in many different contexts.

While we teach in this one moment of history, we are a part of what has gone before us and what will follow us. What we know of the Christian faith we received from others who have learned before us; what future generations will know of the Christian faith is what we currently teach them. To honor our heritage and to preserve for posterity, we must take seriously our role in teaching and learning.

This book builds upon the premise that the goal of Christian teaching is for learning to occur in the life of the individual. We teach in ways that are best for the learner. Both the learner and the teaching process are to be valued.

The idea of the passport is used in presenting this work. A passport provides the essential documentation needed for travel. The passport, along with appropriate visas, allows individuals to visit various parts of the world. You obtain your basic passport from the material presented in part 1, the foundations for all teaching and learning. Part 1 may be called the "who, what, how, and why" of teaching/learning. Chapters in part 1 deal with the biblical basis of teaching/learning, a theory of teaching/learning, the learner, the teacher, lesson planning, and teaching/learning motivation. Each chapter includes sections that establish the importance of the topic; define chapters goals; review of chapter material; and preview of upcoming material. Interspersed among the foundational elements are practical ways of applying the information to everyday situations. Personal learning activities are also included at the end of each chapter.

Part 2, like the visa, deals with specific contexts for Christian teaching/learning. Part 2 may be called the "when and where" of teaching/learning. The chapters in part 2 include information on the Sunday School or Bible teaching program, the worship service, leadership training, missions education, study groups, committees, mission activities, music, and writing. Each chapter contains specific suggestions for utilizing these opportunities for effective teaching/learning. Each chapter also includes sections on establishing the importance of the topic; defining chapter goals; and reviewing the opportunity (context). Additional resources are provided for more information on these specific contexts.

Teaching/learning is a part of our Christian faith. God calls us to be disciples; disciples share their knowledge and faith with those around them. We must recognize and use our opportunities to be redemptive agents in people's lives. That is, we must all be teachers of the Living Word. The following pages will help you to learn how to seize the teaching moments. Once you have seized the moment, the book will tell you what to do with it!

PART I | The Passport to Teaching/Learning Opportunities
or
The Who, What, How, and Why of Teaching/Learning

1. Biblical and Historical Basis of Teaching/ Learning

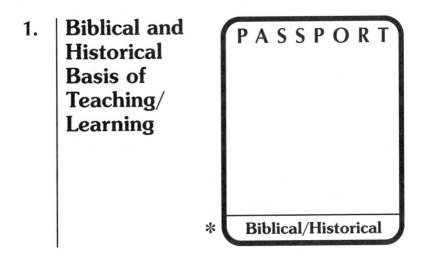

PASSPORT

✳ Biblical/Historical

Establishing Importance

In the beginning was history. At least, it appears that way to readers who discover that most texts begin with a historical overview of the subject. Do writers, editors and publishers begin with history because that is a part of the formula for successful publishing? If not, what is the real purpose behind beginning with history, other than the fact that everybody else does it?

This book begins with history because we are historical creatures and the content of the Christian faith is historical. The very faith demonstrated in our Christian lives has been transmitted through centuries of history, culture, and tradition. We are a product of past experiences. To understand ourselves and the present moment, we must explore the past. Understanding the past can help us interpret and make decisions about the present.

History has the potential for teaching us that we are not alone in concerns we have and decisions we make. Our natural tendency is to be egocentric; we believe that the world begins and ends with us. No one ever cared as much or loved as much as we do. No one was ever consumed with the passion for teaching and learning that we posses. History reveals how mistaken we are.

Christian concerns do not begin and end with us. We are not the first individual or the first generation to ask questions about the teacher, the learner, or the learning methods. These questions have been asked and answered by countless generations before us. To know their answers may help us in approaching the issues of teaching and learning and in arriving at our own tentative solutions. I emphasize *tentative* because each generation must decide for itself how best to proclaim the gospel through teaching and learning opportunities. Methods productive in the 1940s and 50s will not necessarily be productive in the year 2000 and beyond.

In Africa, where I taught, the chief teaching/learning method was lecture. Books were scarce. Learners were eager to write down every word from the mouth of the teacher. How unnerving that each word I taught was being carefully transcribed for future reference. Their carefully written notes became their books in isolated areas. Now, in Texas, my students use computers and study in well-equipped libraries. It is equally frightening when students do not take any notes from my lectures. I place less emphasis upon extensive lectures and more on discussion and projects. In my own life, I have seen the teaching/learning situation vary. What worked in one culture and situation was not the best for another culture and situation.

As we strive for quality Christian teaching and learning in the twentieth and twenty-first centuries, we must look to our roots for direction, strength, and support. By examining our biblical-historical legacy, we become linked with the high priority placed upon Christian teaching/learning. We can then become equipped to answer our own questions on teaching and learning. Keep in mind that we are about to begin a whirlwind tour of some of the highlights of Christian teaching and learning over several thousand years.

Defining Chapter Goals

Now you are going to begin working on your passport to teaching/learning. The first ingredient as previously described is history. By the end of this chapter, you should be able to do the following:
- describe the importance of studying history for present day teaching/learning;
- list various ideas associated with teaching/learning in the Old Testament;
- describe examples of the richness of literary forms in Judeo-Christian literature;

- identify ways the family was involved in education;
- describe the roles of priest, prophets, and sages in education;
- describe the role of the Sabbath in teaching;
- describe the teaching significance of the major Jewish holidays;
- describe how buildings were used as a teaching mechanism;
- identify ways that symbols and ceremonies taught people;
- describe Jesus' method of teaching;
- describe Paul's method of teaching;
- describe the teaching patterns in the New Testament church;
- identify key teaching influences prior to the Reformation;
- describe the Reformation's impact on teaching/learning; and
- summarize present-day insights gained from studying the biblical and historical basis of teaching/learning.

Teaching/Learning in the Old and New Testaments

Various terms may be found in biblical materials that relate to teaching and learning. Examining briefly just the definitions gives insight to the meaning and depth involved in teaching and learning. At least nine different terms are used in the Old Testament and seven terms in the New Testament with regard to teaching/learning.[1] These terms provide various insights into teaching/learning. Old Testament meanings include disciplining in life's activities; casting forth new ideas; instructing in the ways of God; illuminating truth; seeing spiritual reality; instructing, persuading, and admonishing; and protecting and nurturing out of devotion, ownership, and responsibility. New Testament ideas include holding a discourse; causing one to learn; placing beside the learner; interpreting information; revealing hidden and secret ideas; being a spokesman; and tending a flock. Two of these ideas, *causing one to learn* and *placing beside the learner,* may need more explanation. *Causing one to learn* means that the idea behind teaching is learning. *Placing beside the learner* means delivering information in a way accessible to the learner. These ideas surrounding teaching/learning are more significant than simply repeating information.

Various structures, such as methods, people, material, and occasions, existed in the ancient world for the teaching/learning process. Each structure provided the framework for communicating spiritual truth both directly and indirectly. While these structures existed centuries ago, their influence continues today. The following types of structures enhanced and influenced the teaching/learning process.

Literature

Prior to the writing of the Old and New Testaments, religious truth and instruction was passed orally from father to son. These early nomadic societies of such men as Abraham and Isaac depended upon the faith being passed down through family tradition. Imagine sitting around a camp fire and hearing your father talk about his experiences with God. Eventually his story became your story to share with your own children. As societies became literate, less mobile, and more numerous in size, religious truth was recorded. Dependence shifted from the oral tradition to the written word. These carefully preserved and transmitted manuscripts became the Old and New Testaments and were the basis of religious curriculum and instruction.

Rich in literary message, the Bible contains various mechanisms by which God's redemption is communicated. The various divisions of the Bible give insight into the complexity and majesty of the teaching/learning process. The Torah, or Law, the first five books of the Old Testament, was the first literature of the Hebrews. In these early volumes the meaning and purpose of life is explored and shared with all generations. The story of creation, the fall of mankind, the destruction of the world, God's repopulating the world, the call of Abraham, the children of the Promise, the plight of the Hebrew slaves, the deliverance of the Hebrew children, the giving of the Ten Commandments, the wandering in the wilderness, and the rules of worship and life are recorded in these books. The literature gave an early description of the identity of the Hebrew people.

Additional volumes of history continue to describe Hebrew destiny: Joshua, Judges, Ruth, 1 and 2 Samuel, 1 and 2 Kings, 1 and 2 Chronicles, Ezra, Nehemiah, and Esther. This carefully recorded history was the history of how God worked in the lives of His people. The hand of God was seen and recorded for all generations. While prose or narrative was often the medium of the message, poetry was also used to convey truth. Using poetical devices, God's message is captured both in the prophets and in the books of Job, Psalms, Proverbs, Ecclesiastes, Song of Solomon, and Lamentations. These volumes contain songs of praise, laments of grief, confession, intense drama, wisdom, and love. The truth in this form is just as true as that found in the narratives. The narrative, "In the beginning when God created the heavens and the earth" (Gen. 1:1) and the poem or song "The mighty one, God the Lord, speaks and summons the earth from the rising of the sun to its setting" (Ps. 50:1) are both testimonies to the power and supremacy of God.

The Bible continues its variety with the firey message of the prophets in leading the people to genuine repentance and righteous living. The four major prophets are Isaiah, Jeremiah, Daniel, and Ezekiel. These prophets were real people with the same convictions, emotions, struggles, strengths, and weaknesses that we have today. The prophet Isaiah received his call to ministry during a period of discouragement while in the Temple (Isa. 6). Born into a priestly family, the prophet Jeremiah demonstrated the fervent belief in his call to ministry and his continual objections to that call (Jer. 1:5-6; 14:17-18; 20:7,9,14-18). Because of his ministry, Jeremiah was often cut off from normal social functions, such as weddings, funerals, and feasts (Jer. 15:17; 16:5,8).

Taken as a captive, young Daniel was another key leader in the Jewish exile in Babylon. The book that bears his name provides words of encouragement regarding God's sovereignty. The forces of evil will ultimately be defeated. Another Jewish exile, Ezekiel, broke with popular theology by proclaiming that God was God, even in Babylon. God was not limited to the geography of Palestine. God was with His people in the exile (Ezek. 1:3-4). These prophets were living, breathing, and teaching examples. God used many different people of various personalities and backgrounds to teach and lead His people.

Another category of writing in the Old Testament is the Minor Prophets. These prophets, termed *minor* by length of the works and not by their importance, include Hosea, Joel, Amos, Obadiah, Jonah, Micah, Nahum, Habakkuk, Zephaniah, Haggai, Zechariah, and Malachi. Like the major prophets, these minor prophets used numerous teaching devices such as question and answer, object lessons, courtroom drama and dramatic monologue. The prophets provide dramatic, never dull, insights into the character of God and His people. Hosea bought his wife back from slavery and restored her former position of honor—symbolic of God's active redemption of His people. Amos used the everyday object of a plumb line (Amos 7:7-9) to illustrate how God's people must measure and secure its foundation. The story of Jonah tells of one who tried to escape God's plan and found it impossible to run away from God. By word and by deed, God used the prophets to teach Israel of Himself.

With this rich legacy contained in the Old Testament, the Jews were especially concerned with the keeping of the law. Further commentary developed in order to explain the primary literature (Old Testament). After the Babylonian captivity in 597 B.C., various commentaries on the Law developed. The Talmud consists of a host of literature that included interpretations of keeping the Torah. Additional writings include the Haggadah, a manual on observing the various feasts, and the Halakah, a treatise on legal decisions.

Serious about the instruction of their young in sacred Scripture, the faithful Jews required their young to memorize lengthy portions of Scripture. Memorization included the Shema (Deut. 6:4-9), the Hallel (Pss. 5:113-118), Levitical law (Lev. 1-8), and a personal text of Scripture. Knowing the law and keeping the law were synonymous. After studying the Torah as a young child, the Jewish youth advanced to study the Talmud. Various gifted youth often associated with one particular teacher or rabbi.

Beginning in the New Testament world of the first century, the various Gospel accounts and letters to the newly established churches were recorded. These materials became the basis for instruction in the early church. Like the Old Testament, the New Testament is rich in literary style and teaching/learning devices.

One primary device is the personalization of the message for the hearers. The four Gospels portray Christ with special emphases to various religious and cultural groups. Matthew was written to the Jewish community with a rich background and expectation in tradition; Mark, to the Roman community with an emphasis on action and conquest; Luke, to the Gentile community lacking in Jewish religious upbringing; and John, to a Hellenistic world of culture, philosophy and art. While the same Jesus Christ is proclaimed, the message is targeted to various audiences, depending upon their background, experience, and maturity. The gospel message becomes a personal message for all individuals.

This deep personalization is characteristic of the New Testament. The book of Acts continues to portray the rich historical work of the Holy Spirit in the lives of new converts and newly established churches. Like current religious newspapers, it shows what God was doing in the lives of people and churches.

Addressing current issues, needs, and controversies is a part of the New Testament teaching/learning. Issues included the subjects of marriage, divorce, family relationships, obedience to the state, slavery, ministry with the less fortunate, turmoil in churches, false teachers, and political (religious) parties. These topics can still be found in today's newspapers, motion pictures, and television programs. Listed in their order in the Bible, thirteen letters comprise the Pauline Epistles: Romans, 1 and 2 Corinthians, Galatians, Ephesians, Philippians, Colossians, 1 and 2 Thessalonians, 1 and 2 Timothy, Titus, and Philemon. These works addressed specific needs, situations, and people in the growing New Testament churches. As Paul came to the end of his life and ministry, he instructed Timothy to "continue in what you have learned and firmly believe, knowing from whom you learned it" (2 Tim. 3:14) and "carry out your ministry" (2 Tim. 4:5). Fulfilling any ministry involves teaching others about redemption in Christ.

While Paul is a primary writer to the early churches, other leaders wrote and encouraged the early churches. Listed in their order in the Bible, the General Letters include Hebrews, James, 1 and 2 Peter, 1, 2, and 3 John, and Jude. These letters address specific situations and give admonitions for the Christian life. The last book of the New Testament is the book of Revelation. Written as apocalyptic literature (intended to reveal God's truth), Revelation offers hope to Christians facing persecution. Highly symbolic, the message of Revelation is God's ultimate victory in the world.

These New Testament writings were circulated to various churches scattered throughout the known world. These writings formed the Canon of the New Testament and by the second century A.D., the Bible (Old and New Testament) was the basis for Christian teaching/learning. The Word, both written and oral, and in many different forms, was foundational for Christian teaching/learning.

Family

In biblical thought and practice, the primary responsibility for instruction was with the family. Both father and mother shared the task of the training of children. Parents taught their children the basic skills needed for survival in their world, such as how to find water, to find and prepare food, to care for the sick, and to make shelter. Children often followed in their family occupation, such as farming, shepherding, or commerce. Children learned these skills with "on the job training" opportunities. Regardless of the mundaneness of the training, it was considered a God-given responsibility and opportunity.

Children receive training not only in survival skills but also in religious education. Being a responsible member of society was important; equally important was service to God. Regarded as a gift from God, children were to receive instruction in the way in which they should live. Education consisted of telling and retelling the history of the family, the tribe, and involved home religious ceremonies.

In these family activities, the child would ask a question and the father would respond. For example, in the Passover observance, the child might ask, "Father, why do we eat the bitter herb?" The father would reply, "To remind us of the time when we were held captive in Egypt." These ceremonies vividly impressed upon the child his relationship to the larger family of Israel. Each person was called to be a part of the community of faith. Faith was taught in the family through living example, participation, questions, and ceremony.

Priests

God gave the priests the far-reaching responsibility of instructing the people in holy worship and holy living. The priests from the tribe of Levi (the tribe of Moses) were to lead the Hebrew nation in becoming a nation of priests. The priests assumed various roles in the fulfillment of this sacred task. The priests were involved in the offering of various temple sacrifices; the healing of disease; judging in controversies; and instructing in the Torah. These priests had multiple, not simplistic, ministries as they carried out the work of God.

In time the priesthood developed its own hierarchy with levels and classifications of priestly duties. The rigors of purity were inherent in the priesthood. Holiness of the priesthood expressed itself in various fashions, such as the admonition against touching the dead, restrictions regarding marriage, and the need to remain clean, especially during religious ceremonies. Not given any particular land as were the other tribes, the priests were scattered throughout the land of Canaan and were to be supported by the offerings of the people. While they were to live everywhere and to perform multiple ministries, they were all to remain pure in purpose before God.

Like other religious groups and institutions, the priesthood lost its purity and fell victim to corruption which is often characteristic of organizations and institutions. Priests who sought to lead others in the worship of God often failed to lead in their own families. An early example was the priest Eli who failed to discipline his own sons. Because of their greed and lustful actions, Phinehas and Hophni, Eli's sons, shamed their father and brought disgust to the worshipers of God (1 Sam. 2:12-36). The great prophet Samuel served with Eli and doubtlessly watched Eli's failure to discipline his sons. Interestingly, Samuel also failed to discipline his own sons (1 Sam. 8:1-3). The modeling done by religious leaders can be felt by succeeding generations who follow their example.

Self-interest, corruption, and ritualism often characterized the priest and, in turn, the nation. Accounts in the last chapter of Judges illustrate the corruption of the priesthood. Two revolting incidents are portrayed: a Levite who prostitutes his office to erect idolatrous images (vv. 17-18); and a Levite who gives his concubine/wife for the sexual pleasures of men to spare himself from their own homosexual advances (vv. 19-21). As the priests fell in their devotion to God, so fell others of the nation. After years of neglect and corruption, the priesthood ceased to fulfill its mission.

The prophets proclaimed that the priests had failed to provide the essential religious instruction and admonition. Malachi 2:7-9 states: "For the lips of a priest should guard knowledge, and people should seek instruction from his mouth, for he is the messenger of the Lord of hosts. But you have turned aside from the way; you have caused many to stumble by your instruction; you have corrupted the covenant of Levi, says the Lord of hosts, and so I make you despised and abased before all the people, in as much as you have not kept my ways but have shown partiality in your instruction." Failing to keep pure in example, the priests lost their opportunity for service.

Prophets

The prophets' primary role was bringing God's Word to His people. The message of the prophets was practical: people must turn from their sins and return to God. The prophets proclaimed just and righteous living and condemned meaningless religious ceremonies. While their basic message was the same, their approach in teaching was as individualized as they were.

The prophets emerged from every corner of the land of Canaan and from every social class and vocation. They came from such varying backgrounds as the farmer/ shepherd (Amos) to the prince of the court (Isaiah). Despite differences in background, each prophet had a common mission. Because of uniqueness of background and experience, each prophet was able to reach a certain segment of the population. Why not just one type of prophet or one formula for the prophet's role? Simple enough, there are many different people and situations. No one person can minister to all types of people. The Bible does not portray only one model for teaching God's Word.

While proclaiming the message of God was primary, the prophets participated in the community with various roles. The prophets periodically assumed the role of counselor, such as David's consultation of the court prophet Nathan. Often prophets, such as Amos, delivered oracles without being asked. Some prophets became highly involved in politics and influenced international and national development. The prophets were at times able to predict the future. Jeremiah predicted the fall of Jerusalem and the return from Babylonian captivity. Both Micah and Isaiah predicted the birth of the Messiah. Most significantly, the prophets were involved in pleading for the helpless, the homeless, the orphaned, the oppressed, and the widowed. The prophets were people involved in their community. The prophets saw faith in God as actively involving all the pursuits and interests of mankind.

In many instances, the prophets chose symbolic acts to teach and dramatize their spoken words. For example, Ahijah tore his garment into twelve pieces and bid Jeroboam to take ten of them. The ten pieces symbolized God's giving Jeroboam ten tribes (1 Kings 11:29-32). These objects or visual aids enhanced and secured the attention of the hearers. For the discerning listener, the tearing of the cloth symbolized the tearing of the nation. Such vivid images would remain long with the hearer as they watched the disintegration of the nation. The prophets also engaged in the working of miracles. Elijah caused a jar of meal and container of oil not to be depleted for the widow of Zarephath (1 Kings 17:8-16), and he cured Naamam. In addition to securing initial attention, these miracles displayed the active power of God in events and in people's lives.

Regardless of their activities, the prophets observed God working through the history of His people, taught people through various dramatic devices, used their unique opportunities for teaching different groups, and proclaimed the need for righteous living with God.

Sages

Another group in the Old Testament teaching arena were the sages or wise men. Little information is known about this group. They appear to have been older men of the community recognized for their wisdom. Primarily concerned with instructing and encouraging the youth in godly living, the sages drew upon their maturity and experiences to provide practical insights into current problems. Rather than focusing exclusively on the past, the sages used past insights and wisdom to help in current situations. Their contributions were highly practical and pertinent. Unfortunately, their influence waned as the Greek culture with its emphasis on worldly wisdom threatened the nation's spiritual vitality during the interbiblical period. The richness of wisdom gained from experience in godly living was abandoned in favor of mental speculation.

Sabbath

A primary teaching structure for the Hebrews was the Sabbath, a day that involved instruction with the focus being placed upon God's love and the study of His Word. The observance of this day, unlike the other days of the week, was set aside for rejuvenation and enrichment. Just as God rested from His labors, people were to rest from their labors and to reflect upon what God had done.

The activities of the Sabbath were limited, and work was suspended. This day was to be different from the other days of the week. No longer preoccupied with the toil of everyday life, the people were to worship and to learn of their God. Even meals were considered important as the people ate specially prepared foods on the Sabbath. The Sabbath and its activities were vivid reminders of God's creation and His setting apart of Israel for a holy purpose. By observing the Sabbath, a cycle (six days of work, a day of rest) was produced in which people worked and yet they remembered their God in their experience. Teaching and learning occurred as they took time to reflect upon their experiences.

Later the Sabbath became a weighty and technical obligation, rather than a joyous time. Laws developed in regard to keeping the Sabbath holy. These laws often defined labor that must be avoided such as planting, plowing, reaping, tying a knot, writing two letters, putting out a fire, and removing items from one house to another. The rabbis compiled a list of thirty-nine categories of labor defined as work. When criticized for working by feeding His followers, Jesus responded, "The sabbath was made for humankind, and not humankind for the sabbath" (Mark 2:27). What was intended for joy had been reduced to a burden.[2] Nevertheless, the practice of the Sabbath taught powerfully what was acceptable and nonacceptable behavior.

Holidays

In Hebrew faith and practice, special holidays and observances existed which commemorated significant events in the life history of the Hebrew nation. Three major feasts characterized the Jewish calendar.

Each feast possessed a special religious and agricultural significance. The Pesoach or Passover (Ex. 12:1-28) was celebrated in the spring and marked the barley harvest. Religiously the Passover represented the redemption or deliverance from Egyptian captivity. Shovouos or Pentecost (Ex. 23:16; Lev. 23:15-22) was celebrated in the summer and marked the wheat harvest. Pentecost commemorated the giving of the Law on Mount Sinai. Sukkoth or the Festival of the Tabernacles (Lev. 23:40-44) was celebrated in the fall and marked the grape harvest. Religiously, Sukkoth signified the forty years of wandering in the desert. In addition to the feasts and festival, various holy days were observed.

Two major holy days characterized the Jewish year. Yom Kippur or the Day of Atonement dealt with the sins of the past year. This observation involved fasting and repentance. Rosh Hashanah, the Day of Judgment, was celebrated at the beginning of the Jewish New Year. The new year was approached with a contrite heart. Observing these holy days involved repenting, requesting God's mercy, and performing good deeds.

Three minor holy days were observed. Observed with fasting, the Ninth day of Av or Tishah-b'Av mourned the destruction of the Temple and Jerusalem. Chanukah or the Festival of Lights commemorated the successful revolt of the Macabees against Antiochus Epiphanes. Purim, the Feast of Esther, celebrated the deliverance of the Jews from their enemy, Haman.

These feasts and holy days were rich in history and teaching. On these days, the family and the community celebrated significant events in their history. The feasts and holy days were concrete reminders and teachers of the Hebrew faith and pilgrimage.[3] The God who called the Chosen People into existence was not forgotten, nor was their place and responsibility in history forgotten. These observances brought entire families and communities together in purpose and spirit. While there was a basis in celebrating agricultural accomplishment (a necessity for Jewish life), there was also the observance of God's active involvement in life. Without God, the fruit of the harvest was not possible. God was remembered as the One who makes life possible and meaningful. Life evolved around remembering the continual work of God.

Buildings

Buildings provided the common meeting ground for teaching/learning/ worship to occur and also provided, through design and furnishings, a teaching/learning environment. Three buildings serving a primary role in Hebrew life were the tabernacle, the temple, and the synagogue.

Tabernacle.—The tabernacle was a temporary, portable dwelling place of God. The tabernacle was constructed during the wandering of the Hebrews prior to entering the promised land. Just as they were without a permanent home as a people, they were without a permanent worship center. Where they sojourned, the tabernacle sojourned.

The design of the tabernacle and its furniture was highly significant. The innermost part of the tabernacle, known as the holy of holies, contained the ark of the covenant. Overlaid with gold, the ark was a chest made of fine acacia wood. The chest contained the Ten Commandments. Only on the Day of Atonement could the high priest enter the holy of holies with the task of making atonement for the sins of the people. A veil separated the holy of holies, maintained in darkness, from the rest of the tabernacle. The presence of God dwelt in the holy of holies. Man approached God indirectly through the intercession of priests. Later with the death of Christ, the veil separating the holy of holies from the outside was torn (Matt. 27:51). God instituted a new way of relationship with God—directly through the redemptive work of Christ. Believers now go directly to God without an intermediary.

The outer chamber of the tabernacle consisted of the table of shewbread, lampstands, and an altar of incense. The twelve cakes which the priests ate each sabbath were placed on the table of shewbread. Representative of the twelve tribes, these cakes served as symbols of gratitude and commitment to God. The lampstands represented Israel's call to be a people of light. The sweet-smelling incense burned on the altar of incense, representing the continual life and fervency of prayer. The tabernacle in theological design played a part in teaching the nature and character of God and of humankind.

Temple.—The basic design, furnishings, and theology of the tabernacle were reproduced in the temple. When the nation of Israel was firmly established in the land of Canaan, David wished to make a permanent temple to replace the tabernacle of the wilderness. However, through the prophet Nathan, God forbade David to build the temple (2 Sam. 7:5ff). The task and privilege of building the temple fell to David's son, Solomon. Solomon's Temple took seven years to build and was complete in approximately 1005 B.C. Although the dimensions were different, the arrangement of the temple was identical with that of the tabernacle (1 Kings 5:1-13). After Solomon's death, the nation was divided into two nations with the northern kingdom known as Israel and the southern kingdom known as Judah. Israel fell to the Assyrians in 722-721 B.C. Judah survived approximately two hundred years longer but fell to the Babylonian army in 586-587 B.C. Jerusalem, the capital of Judah, was destroyed, and Solomon's temple lay in ruins.

In 538 B.C., under the edict of Cyrus, the Jews in Babylonian captivity were permitted to return to their native land of Canaan. One of their religious desires was to rebuild the temple. A new temple was built under the leadership of Zerubbabel. Although it took twenty-two years to build, Zerubbabel's temple never matched the splendor of Solomon's temple, and the ark of the covenant had been lost.

Later, Zerubbabel's temple was expanded under the direction of Herod the Great, and it was one of great beauty. The outside court of Herod's temple, known as the court of the Gentiles, was as far as Gentiles could come into the temple. It was followed by the court of the women which prohibited any Jewish woman from going any further. Nearer the center of the temple was the court of Israel, where only Jewish men could stand near the great altar. In accordance with the design of Solomon's temple, the holy of holies was beyond the court of Israel. Thus, the Temple continued to teach a hierarchy of approach and accessibility to God. Ceremony and ritual provided a barrier to a direct approach by anyone. The ministry of Jesus Christ altered this inaccessibility to God. Human beings could approach the Father directly through the Son. Like the other temple, Herod's temple and Jerusalem were destroyed in A.D. 70 by the Roman army under Titus.

Synagogues.—Apparently arising during the Babylonian exile, the synagogue served as a community center of worship and study. Often located in the highest point in the area, symbolic of the primacy of God's Word and direction for human life, these synagogues were designed for study for the young and the old. After the destruction of Herod's temple, the synagogues continued to be a site of study and worship. Organized in any community with ten Jewish males present, the synagogues were places of prayer, study, preaching, and teaching. The highest officer of the synagogue was the rabbi or teacher. Originally meeting only on the Sabbath and feast days, the people extended worship and study to other days of the week. Their worship services included the reading of the Shema, prayers, reading of the Law and Prophets, the sermon, and the benediction. Worship and study became an increasing part of everyday life for the Jews.

In the New Testament era, Christian believers continued to meet in the synagogues. When driven out of the synagogues, the believers met in homes. Later, Christians built their own buildings for worship and study. Much of early worship and study in the church was patterned after that of the synagogues.

Symbols and Ceremonies

Everyday life and practices provided opportunities for teaching/learning in the world of the Old and New Testaments. Various clothing and other ornaments reminded individuals of their need for and responsibility to God. The tallith worn by men, for example, was a prayer shawl with fringes. The phylactery, a band attached to a small box containing portions of the Law, was worn on the head or inner left arm to remind the wearer and others of the importance of God's Law. The mezuzah, a small container holding a small parchment scroll inscribed with passages found in Deuteronomy 6:4-9 and 11:13-21, was attached to the doorposts of buildings.

In the subsequent years in the Christian world, the sign of the fish became a symbol of Christian brotherhood and safety. Translated from the Greek word "icthus" meaning fish, the term is an acrostic meaning "Jesus Christ, God's Son, Savior." It was an early Christian statement of faith. Often drawn in the sand, the fish became a secretive way of identifying other believers.

Basic ceremonies for everyday life and special religious occasions were important in Hebrew faith. Before meals, prayers of thanksgiving were offered. Certain ceremonies, such as the rites of circumcision for Jewish males on the eighth day of life, signified their part in the Jewish community. The bar mitzvah was a ceremony which celebrated the thirteen year old males' entrance into the adult Hebrew community. The young male would recite portions of Scripture and assume adult responsibility for faith and practice. Teaching and learning occurred through the practices of such ceremonies and rituals.

In the New Testament world, baptism became the chief symbol of entrance into the Christian faith. Along with baptism, observance of the common meal or the Lord's Supper marked the remembrance of what was done and what was ahead. Both baptism and the Lord's Supper contributed to the teaching and the learning of the early church. In observing the act of baptism, both the individual being baptized and those people witnessing that baptism re-lived, in a sense, their own personal faith and entrance into a life of discipleship. The importance of fellowship, the common bond of faith, and the hope of Christ's promises were taught each time the Lord's Supper was observed.

Teaching Personalities in the New Testament

Jesus Christ

The primary teaching personality in the New Testament is Jesus Christ. Two core teaching credentials of Jesus may be summarized by the two words *authority* and *relationship*. First, Jesus spoke with the authority as the Son of God, and His teaching was recognized as one of authority (Matt. 8:29). His own authority emerged from His relationship with the Father and His submission to the will of the Father. Jesus shared His authority with His followers, His disciples.

By sharing His authority, Jesus invited His disciples to become a part of the life-long teaching/learning process in Christian discipleship. He gave authority to His disciples as they were involved in ongoing ministry (Luke 9:1-2). This shared authority continues in the lives of disciples today as we are given the Word to teach and to preach. By proclaiming the Christian message, we are offering individuals an opportunity to believe. Through the Word and testimony of the Holy Spirit, belief is possible. What privilege and responsibility! Caution must be exercised; authority must not be abused. Authority comes from our relationship and submission to God.

Second, relationships formed the context out of which Jesus taught. Jesus loved people and showed interest in their individual needs. He taught love for God as He showed love for people. Ultimately His love for humanity resulted in His own death; through His death, each person has the potential for eternal life.

Variety and diversity were characteristic of Jesus' teaching approach. Rather than focusing exclusively on the large crowd, Jesus focused attention upon small groups of individuals, such as the twelve disciples and the inner circle of Peter, James, and John. With these disciples, He focused upon intensive teaching/learning experiences. Jesus employed a variety of teaching/learning methods, such as the use of parables. The one of the sower and the merchant is an example. Through the use of questions, Jesus challenged people to answer exactly who He was. His use of the mustard seed to illustrate faith was an object lesson. Field experiences, such as going out teaching, preaching, and healing, provided opportunity to put what was learned into practice. Jesus also taught through more lengthy discourses, such as the Sermon on the Mount. Further exploration of Jesus's teaching and subsequent teaching implications will be developed in later chapters.

Noted pastor and teacher Calvin Miller proscribed Jesus's teaching method:

> His target was not human intellect but salvation, morality, relationship and destiny. Collectively, these subjects fill His teachings—to learn from Him does not make one smarter as studying trigonometry or literature might. To learn from Jesus makes one moral, contextual and hopeful; the sum of these three integers is meaning.[4]

More often referred to as a rabbi or teacher than as preacher, Jesus nurtured and taught His disciples. Jesus spoke, "You call me Teacher and Lord—and you are right, for that is what I am" (John 13:13). The teaching/learning that Jesus offered continued even beyond His earthly life and death. Comforting and guiding His disciples, Jesus said: "I still have many things to say to you, but you cannot bear them now. When the Spirit of truth comes, he will guide you into all the truth; for he will not speak on his own, but will speak whatever he hears, and he will declare to you the things that are to come" (John 16:12-13).

Paul

The second great teaching personality of the New Testament is Paul. Born Saul of Tarsus, Paul was highly trained in Jewish faith and practice. After his conversion from being a persecutor of Christians to being a follower of Christ, Paul focused his energy and intellect on preaching and teaching the Christian faith.

Paul's teaching ministry took an additional dimension than that of Jesus. Although a preacher and teacher, Paul taught extensively as a writer whose works were spread throughout the known world. Paul instructed those who already possessed faith in Christ and those who would yet possess that faith. His teaching and writing focused not only to the concerns of his immediate generation but also to future generations. Much of our knowledge regarding Christ and the church are through Paul's writings in the New Testament.

Variety marked the life of this great teacher, preacher, and writer. Paul taught in a variety of settings—in cities, in the country, on a ship, in humble villages, in the capital city of Rome, and in prison. Paul used illustrations that would appeal to many individuals of varying experiences and backgrounds. To the Jews, he showed how Christ was the fulfillment of the Hebrew Scriptures. He compared living the Christian life to that of an athlete running a race. To those well-versed in philosophy, Paul was able to communicate effectively. Scripture records that "I [Paul] have become all things to all people, that I might by all means save some (1 Cor. 9:22b)." Paul had an awareness of reaching people. Reaching, to Paul, involved doing what was necessary that people might be taught the gospel. Such a life-commitment characterizes sound Christian teaching/learning.

Teachers today can learn much about teaching through the lives of Jesus and Paul. Jesus' commitment and relationship to the Father should be characteristic of Christian teachers. Like Jesus, teachers should form relationships that allow for life-changing teaching to occur. Like Paul, we should be aware of the whole world as we seek to give a Christian witness. Variety in approach and methodology is critical as we deal with a variety of human need. While there is one gospel to be taught and preached, there are many ways to accomplish it.

The Church

Under the direction of Paul and the other disciples, the early church had numerous opportunities for teaching/learning. Wherever the church gathered, teaching occurred. At Antioch of Syria, the didaskalos (teacher), an office within the church, was first used. Highly cosmopolitan in arts, literature, commerce, and religion, Antioch was one of the most influential cities in the Roman World, and the name "Christian" was first applied there to followers of Jesus (Acts 11:26). In addition, Antioch was the center of the missionary movement of the early church.

It is not surprising that the office of teaching at Antioch is related to the missionary enterprise (Acts 13:1). Christian development demands that the gospel be shared with others. Thus, as the word was taught, the young converts saw the necessity of sharing the Word with the world. Later, teaching became more a part of an official function of the church, rather than a natural outflow of belief. *The Didache* or *The Teaching of the Twelve Apostles*, a non-canonical work of the late first century, was a popular manual for the guidance of religious teachers. *The Didache* contained information on preparing catechumens (candidates for church membership) for baptism, information on worship, duties of church officers, and exhortations to remain faithful.

Various types of teaching existed within the early church, including Christian interpretation of Hebrew Scriptures; the teaching of the gospel; evangelism with a focus upon commitment to Christ; the life and teachings of Jesus; and teaching ethical choices that Christians faced.[5] By examining the types of teaching conducted, several conclusions can be drawn about their approach to curriculum. First, focus was given to both the Old Testament and the New Testament. Second, the person of Jesus was preeminent in their teaching. Third, people were encouraged in their personal commitment to Christ. Fourth, people were encouraged to make ethical choices with their Christian values. Thus, the curriculum was historical, personal, everyday-oriented and centered in Jesus Christ. Three types of instructional meetings existed where these materials were often taught: the preaching service; the common meal, usually followed by the Lord's Supper; and the business meeting.[6] Teaching and learning occurred wherever and whenever the church met.

As new converts were brought into the early Christian church, specialized study and schools developed for admitting the catechumen into church membership. Although instruction was basic, the process lasted between two and three years. The form of instruction was primarily catechetical—question and answer. For example, the question may be asked, "Who is Jesus?" A memorized answer would then follow. Individuals became increasingly trained for church membership in this two-three year period. Those desiring church membership paid a price through commitment and discipline.

As the Roman Empire disintegrated, learning across Europe became less and less prominent. The majority of people were uneducated, and often the clergy were unlearned. What occurred culturally or socially in Europe influenced the education within the church. Gradually, the extensive training required for church membership vanished. In part, the new church members were coming not as adult baptisms but as infant baptisms. Theological beliefs about children and baptism influenced educational practice.

The teaching/learning process for the majority of the church was conducted primarily through religious drama known as mystery plays and through the worship services of the church. The ability to read and to have access to Scripture was a rarity. The majority of the western clergy did not read the biblical languages of Greek and Hebrew. The Bible, having been translated in Latin by Jerome in the fourth century A.D., was not available to all, and only a few had the privilege to read the Scripture. Although Latin was the official language of the church, few layman spoke Latin. Eventually the language became one heard in church with limited meaning for the average worshiper. Without Bibles of their own and the ability to read the Scriptures, the laymen were dependent upon church leadership for spiritual direction.

Prior to the Protestant Reformation, short-lived attempts were made to educate people. Various monastic schools scattered across Europe gave varying priorities to education. Several political leaders attempted educational changes. Charles the Great (A.D. 747-814), also known as Charlemagne of France, sought to bring about educational reform to the clergy and to the laity. Priests were required to pass literacy examinations and were required to teach those who came for instruction. Charlemagne's educational reforms diminished after his death. Alfred the Great (A.D. 849-899) of England championed educational reform by stressing training for the clergy and the use of the vernacular.[7]

The clergy also often attempted educational reform. John Wycliffe (c. 1329-1384) in England and John Hus (c. 1369-1415) in Czechoslovakia were two pre-reformation personalities who emphasized teaching on the basis of biblical authority in the language of the people. These attempts provided momentary glimpses of light in a European world of darkness.

Only during the subsequent sixteenth-century Protestant Reformation, through the efforts of such reformers as Martin Luther (1483-1546), John Calvin (1509-1564) and John Knox (c. 1513-1572), did the teaching/learning process refocus upon the necessity of biblical instruction for every individual on a wide scale. Bibles were printed in national languages; laymen were taught to read; and laymen were encouraged to read Scripture and to reason for themselves. Lives were changed as Bibles were opened. In reaction to the Protestant Reformation, the Roman Catholic Church began emphasizing its own reading and teaching of Scripture. The Roman Catholic Church established teaching and missionary orders, such as the Jesuits, to combat the heresy of Protestantism and to promote the teachings of the Roman Catholic Church. Both Roman Catholic and Protestant became more acquainted with the Scripture.

With the advancements of a now literate and mobile society, churches assumed once again the missionary mandate to "Go, therefore, and make disciples of all nations, baptizing them in the name of the Father and of the Son and of the Holy Spirit" (Matt. 28:19). Renewed interest in learning for the majority of people occurred with the advent of the printing press and the Protestant Reformation. The exploration of the world encouraged teaching and learning in the new missionary enterprise of the church. In the eighteenth century, the modern Sunday School developed and became an established part of Protestant churches. Today the church has developed highly organized educational units for all ages. Christian education is available from preschool to graduate school.

Looking Back

Today it is hard to imagine a time when churches did not emphasize teaching and learning for all people. However, the opportunity to learn has been a privilege and not always a reality for everyone. In the beginning of this chapter, I pointed out that we are historical people and the Christian faith is a historical one. Too often we think we are the only ones who have dealt with the issues involved in Christian teaching/ learning. We also make the mistake of defining that teaching/learning can only occur in the ways that we have personally seen it practiced. Let us each remember that Christian teaching/learning does not begin and end with us. Christian teaching/learning can occur in ways we have not yet seen.

Hopefully some new insights regarding Christian teaching/learning have emerged as you participated in a brief "grand tour" of Christian history. Let me share with you a few insights that you may have found on your tour.

- The biblical material in its richness, complexity, and majesty is the basis for Christian teaching/learning. To teach creatively and correctly, we should use the variety of methods in which its truths are presented, such as drama, poetry, and exposition. The very presentation methods used in Scripture should be employed in our methods.
- The biblical material should be portrayed as living, not dead, material. Both men and women shared in the unfolding of God's character and plan for people. This material is vibrant because it shows how real men and women experienced the living God.
- The family is a central part of Christian education. What is communicated in the family lays the foundation for character in both godly vocation and life itself. Family ritual and ceremonies are paramount in laying this foundation for faith development.
- God calls the priests and prophets (vocational workers) to multiple ministries that relate to human need. We cannot rightly proclaim

ourselves as teachers if we neglect the needs and concerns of our community. True Christian teaching both shares and lives the faith with others.

- God calls each of us with varying backgrounds, experiences, and opportunities. Christian teaching/learning must nurture the individual as he or she finds a place of leadership and responsibility. God works in many ways through varying personalities in accomplishing His Kingdom.

- Christian teaching/learning must not ignore the importance of the experience of those who have lived godly lives. The mature Christian has a powerful role model to share with others in the faith. Maturity does not come automatically with age but through experience with God. Seek out and learn from those who have faithfully lived the faith.

- Keeping the Sabbath as a time of worship, study, and rest should be a part of our life-style. Caution must be used that we do not exhaust the Sabbath, not with "laws against work," but against busy church activity that does not promote real worship and family time.

- We should use the holidays as a time to teach both our families and communities about our faith in God. Such celebrations should involve meaningful participation by all people.

- In our buildings and homes, we should consider what the structure teaches. Do our churches teach a particular theology by their design and structure? Do we agree with what we may be teaching "structurally"? Where do we spend the greatest part of our resources? Are we building buildings and not building lives? Buildings are important; however, buildings should not be self-centered but should allow each of us to reach out.

- We should carefully evaluate our symbols and ceremonies as legitimate ways of witnessing and teaching the Christian faith. The church has always used symbols; we must use them properly and thoughtfully.

- Christian teaching/learning must nurture both teachers' and learners' relationship to God. Through fellowship with Him, we can fellowship with others and eventually teach with the authority that Christ offers. Our authority emerges from our relationship with Him.

- The early church had many patterns and contexts of teaching. Today the church should have the freedom to teach where people are. Each time the church gathers, the church has opportunity to teach. Variety and freedom should be a natural part of our educational design.

• Christian teaching/learning must help each individual read and think critically for himself about the biblical material. This responsibility is a part of our discipleship. Helping people in discipleship means helping them learn how to think and to act for themselves.

• Genuine Christian teaching/learning has a positive missionary outgrowth. Christian education involves change in our own lives and in our world. Christian teaching does not minister exclusively to itself, but reaches out to others in love.

Looking Ahead

These observations are a few summary insights from examining history. You may have gained others. Think about them; draw conclusions appropriate for your own teaching and learning. Now that you have obtained the first element of your teaching passport, it is time to turn to the second element—a theory of teaching/learning.

Notes

1. "Teach, Teacher, Teaching," Byron H. DeMent, *The International Standard Bible Encyclopedia* (Grand Rapids: Eerdmans, 1939), 2921-2923.

2. See Eugene J. Lipman, *The Mishnah: Oral Teachings of Judaism,* in *B'nai B'rith Jewish Heritage Classics,* (New York: Viking, 1970).

3. See Hayyim Schauss, *The Jewish Festivals: History & Observance* (New York: Schocken, 1938).

4. "Miller," *SBREA Journal* (April-June 1987), 6.

5. Lewis J. Sherrill, *The Rise of Christian Education* (New York: MacMillan, 1944), 144-151.

6. Charles A. Tidwell, *Educational Ministry of a Church* (Nashville: Broadman, 1982), 39.

7. H.G. Good, *A History of Western Education,* 2d ed. (New York: Macmillan, 1960), 73-76.

Learning Activities

1. "Analysis of Instructional Meetings"
   A. Identify the three types of instructional meetings of the early church.
   B. Identify instructional meetings of the church today.

    C. How could meetings today be improved to provide better educational opportunities?

2. "Biblical Teaching Mechanisms"
   List the primary teaching mechanisms of the Old and New Testaments in one column. In the next column, list examples of each of these teaching mechanisms.

3. "Current Teaching Mechanisms"
   List mechanisms today that are used in the learning process in one column. In the next column, give specific examples.

4. "Examining the Gospels"
   Choose any one of the Gospels. Read the Gospel looking for examples of how Jesus taught. List the types of teaching methods illustrated.

5. "Biblical View of Teaching"
   In your own words, describe the Old and New Testament views of teaching.

6. "Training in Church Membership"
   In the early church, candidates for church membership underwent a period of training for two-three years. Identify current educational practices for new church members. How could current practices be improved?

7. "What if ...."
   What would happen if teaching the Christian faith were forbidden? Describe the possible results.

8. "The Basics—Learn and Teach"
   List elements of faith that you believe must be learned and taught.

9. "A Personal Christian Calendar"
   Create a Christian calendar of special occasions. What are the special holidays that should be celebrated? Include ways that the church and home can celebrate and worship together during these special times.

2. | A Theory of Teaching/ Learning

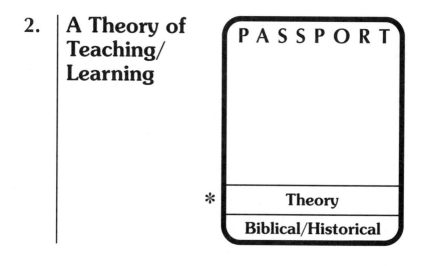

PASSPORT

* Theory

Biblical/Historical

Establishing Importance

Theory is important. How often have we heard that idea? Whether it is in playing the piano, building a house, preparing a meal, or writing a composition, theory is indeed significant. Behind each of these activities is a plan or a pattern of action. A theory is a set of assumptions or beliefs that we have about an idea or an activity. Theories can be simple or complex; however, we cannot escape theories. We all possess them for our various endeavors. Let us examine an activity for which we all have some type of theory—cooking.

I learned the importance of theory and cooking as a young single missionary to Africa. Having never learned to cook, I had previously relied heavily upon packaged foods and frozen meals. Once in Africa I discovered that packaged foods and frozen meals were nonexistent. What was I to do? Starve? Fortunately I had good friends who cooked and who fed me. Had I known the theory behind the preparation of food, I would have been able to improvise in a new setting. What I had learned was one simple way of doing something such as opening a can, rather than the theory behind food preparation such as starting from scratch. At the end of my two-year stay, I had learned at least a dozen ways to use canned corn beef, ranging from barbecued corn beef, corn-beef burgers, and corn-beef spaghetti, to corn beef meatloaf. At least, I had learned a little theory that translated into various foods with varying degrees of taste.

Theory provides procedures for doing. Simply stated, theory is the guiding purpose or idea behind any endeavor. Whether or not it is clearly understood by the practitioner, it is a model pattern that directs and shapes any activity. Theories are powerful forces in teaching and learning situations. All teachers have some theories that guide how they teach others to learn.

A quality theory of teaching involves a quality view of learning. You cannot teach effectively if you do not have a clear understanding of the basic learning process. Teaching seeks to bring about some change in the learner's knowledge, understanding, attitudes, behaviors, and skills. To create change of any type, you must know how the learner learns, then you can plan appropriate teaching/learning strategies. Teaching and learning are two parts of a simultaneous process.

Defining Chapter Goals

As you continue to secure your passport to teaching and learning, it is necessary to develop a theory of teaching/learning. In this review of theory, the following elements or topics will be explored: relationship, feedback, understandable language, sense experience, variety, relevancy/application, interest/attention, modeling, competency, active involvement, environment, and the Holy Spirit. Each of these elements must be viewed from two perspectives: the learner and the teacher. By exploring these two perspectives in both theory and application, a more comprehensive understanding of the entire educational process can be achieved. Once you have developed your theory, you are on your way to the various destinations in Christian education. At the conclusion of this chapter, you should be able to do the following:

- defend the importance of relationships in teaching/learning;
- describe the significance of feedback in the educational process;
- describe the power of language in teaching/learning;
- summarize the impact of sense experience in teaching/learning;
- identify the contributions of variety to teaching/learning;
- demonstrate how to achieve relevancy and application in education;
- explain the relationship between interest and attention in teaching/learning;

- defend the importance of proper modeling in Christian education;
- describe what is involved in competency in teaching/learning;
- demonstrate ways to actively involve the learner;
- identify the elements of a good learning environment; and
- explain the role of the Holy Spirit in Christian education.

Relationship

In one of my favorite novels, *Gone With The Wind*, Scarlett's father reminds his daughter that land is the only thing that lasts, the only thing worth fighting for. While land may last, from both a Christian and a learning perspective, relationships have more eternal significance than a plot of acreage. In fact, relationships are worth fighting for; relationships are the only things that last.

Created by a relational God, mankind is relational. People are made for a wide set of relationships; the central one is responding to God. Additionally, people have the capacity for relationships with each other. Consequently in a teaching/learning situation, the relationship between teacher and learner is crucial. The quality of the relationship can either strengthen or weaken the teaching/learning process.

Adults in church illustrate clearly the importance and significance of relationships in learning. Adult departments are often noted for their unwillingness to promote or to move into an older group with a new teacher and new class members. Somehow the relationships among class members and their teacher are special. People are reluctant to give up such secure learning relationships for uncertain ones. Adult learners are often hesitant to promote as individuals. They are more likely to promote if several promote at the same time and better still if the entire class promotes. Relationships are important in learning.

In relationships, trust holds the relationship together and encourages learning to occur. Without trust, no learner is willing to put himself at risk to explore the unknown. Teachers gain the trust of the learner by earning it. Mrs. Swope, who has taught a class of adult women for thirty years, gains the trust of the women each week. She does that by arriving on time each Sunday morning, preparing for each lesson, keeping their "secrets" confidential, and admitting when she doesn't know all the answers. As she looks, listens, and ministers to the needs of her class, she earns their trust. Trust is built day-by-day, week-by-week.

Since time is required to build trust in a relationship, Christian teaching involves a long-term investment. Investing time means being available and accessible. It is not enough to say that you are available, you must show people you are. For example, show interest in what the people are discussing, try to understand how they feel, enjoy times of fellowship with the class, and spend time getting to know your learners. Trust and time go hand-in-hand.

I vividly remember the extra minutes I spent as a teenaged Christian with my pastor on the steps of our small church. In those few minutes, which often extended into a half hour or longer, I shared my questions and struggles with him. My pastor was spending time discipling me through a quality relationship. Those moments helped shape me into what I am today. I hope, in some small measure, that I "blessed" him as teacher as he "blessed" me as learner.

While relationships influence what is learned, relationships also influence what is taught. No two classes are the same. As a teacher, I have had some classes that "succeeded" and others that did not. In those classes that "succeeded," I saw myself, either rightly or wrongly, as being more effective in my teaching. When I sensed good teaching moments, I gave myself more intensely to the process. Feeling positive about teaching can help you work harder at teaching. Feeling that you are getting through to your learners energizes your teaching and your enthusiasm. Teaching becomes pure joy.

Jesus' relationships illustrated their importance in teaching and learning. Jesus was unable to do great works in His own hometown because His community did not believe in Him. The relationship of the community with Him hindered His ministry and teaching opportunities. Unwilling people cannot be taught nor discipled. John 1:11: "He came to what was his own, and his own people did not accept him." Contrast this limitation to the message found in John 1:12: "But to all who received him, who believed in his name, he gave power to become children of God." Receiving and believing are relationship terms. If we fail to have a faith relationship with Him, we limit what Jesus can do through us. Those who teach the gospel effectively are those in close relationship with Christ. Not only do relationships influence the interactions between the learner and teacher, but also the interactions between mankind and God.

Relationships produce an important aspect in teaching/learning—self-esteem. Self-esteem is the value that we place upon ourselves. We each have self-esteem, whether it is poor or good, low or high. We learn to value ourselves by how we are valued by others. Those having poor self-esteem typically have been in relationships that were negative, non-encouraging, and sometimes abusive.

This measure of worth we give ourselves influences our entire life. What we feel, what we do, and what we say are guided by how we regard ourselves. How and what we learn are influenced greatly by our self-esteem or self-perception. If I think that I cannot learn, I will not learn. If I believe in myself, I am more apt to learn.

Christian teaching/learning involves relationships that contribute to positive self-esteem. We build self esteem in learners by believing in them, giving them opportunity to perform, listening to their questions, correcting them when correction is needed, and praising them. However, we must not forget that teachers must first have positive self-esteem before they can encourage it in others.

Positive self-esteem for the Christian, whether the teacher or the learner, begins in accepting ourselves as Christ accepts us—our strengths and weaknesses, the good and the ugly. In this acceptance, we treat ourselves as Christ would treat us—with a healthy love and respect. Once we have a positive self-esteem, we can reach out to give the same to others. Positive self-esteem helps in living the golden rule: "Do unto others as you would have others do unto you."

Feedback

In teaching/learning, feedback is receiving information about how well we are teaching or how well we are learning. Feedback is a flow of information from one source to another. We have each received feedback from the time of our birth. When we began to make sounds resembling a human word, our parents gave us praise. Otherwise normally healthy adults, myself included, become ecstatic as their babies make these guttural sounds. This parental joy expressed to babies is a type of feedback to the babies. If we said words that were inappropriate or performed acts that were unacceptable, we received our feedback in the form of a frown, a sideways nod, or even a direct hit on our body. These were additional forms of feedback.

Feedback helps us in gaining knowledge, understanding, attitudes, and skills. Feedback signals to us that we are not alone; we are not isolated in an uncaring and empty world. If we are given feedback, at least one other person is present to give information upon which we can reflect. A mark of caring for the learner, as well as a mark of concern for learning, is giving feedback. Telling the learner how well he is doing indicates care.

Without feedback, we are doomed to repeat the same mistakes. For example, when I learned to type, I made the mistake of lifting my elbows up in the air, rather than having them compressed more by my side. Without feedback from my typing teacher, I might have made that error indefinitely. My effectiveness and endurance as a typist would have been impaired. As I prepared research papers, my teachers gave me feedback about my strengths and weaknesses in composition. When I said something cruel to another child, my teacher helped me understand how it felt to be hurt verbally. Feedback allows us to correct any wrong actions, thoughts, reasoning processes, and attitudes that we have. How do I know I'm doing right or wrong unless I am told?

Feedback operates in a cycle. First, the teacher gives some information. The learner then expresses his own knowledge, understandings, attitudes, and responses to that material. In essence, the learner gives feedback to the teacher. The teacher can then respond with either correction or reinforcement. In addition, the teacher has feedback to evaluate his own effectiveness in communicating the information, attitudes, or skills. As a teacher I may sincerely believe I have communicated one idea when, in fact, the learner may be "hearing" something totally different. Nowhere does this show itself more clearly than during examinations. What I thought was described so clearly in my lecture did not appear nearly as clear in my student's test answers. I'll give the student the benefit of the doubt and assume my lecture was not nearly as clear as I had envisioned. Feedback is not only essential to the learner's learning, but also to the teacher's teaching.

Feedback occurs when we pause to listen and to wait for the learner to respond. Beginning teachers are often afraid of silence. How often have you asked a question with no comment from your class? Do you quickly respond? Do you ask another question in the hopes of clarifying the first question? Do you allow the silence as a time of reflection? The insecure teacher is prone to quickly rephrase the question or to answer the question himself or herself. We don't allow the student to struggle with the "pressure of silence." Each of us must take some time to make sense of our newly acquired information. Do not deny the individual the privilege of struggling in silence. As the silence is broken on the part of the learner, feedback is gained as to what is going on in his mind. The teacher may also gain additional insight into his behavior as a teacher.

The giving and receiving of feedback demands courage from both the teacher and the learner. We may not wish to know what is transpiring in the learners' minds. What if they criticize us? What if they imply we are not clear in our explanation or presentation? What if the learner responds and the teacher or class laughs? If I show what I know, the teacher will know how little I do know. Feedback makes each of us vulnerable. However, vulnerability promotes growth in both persons in the teaching/learning process.

On a spiritual level, God provides us with feedback as we seek Him through the study of Scripture and prayer. God gives us feedback through the work of His Word and His Holy Spirit. Jesus said, "Ask, and it will be given you; search, and you will find; knock, and the door will be opened for you" (Matt. 7:7). If feedback is crucial for our spiritual development, surely it is essential for any other type of development, including educational. Feedback allows for the maturing of both teacher and learner.

Understandable Language

The teaching/learning process must occur in a language that is understandable for the learner. College professors are notorious for speaking in "foreign tongues." These foreign tongues may sound like a thesaurus to young freshmen. Even college professors should remember that teaching is not an opportunity to overwhelm or overburden the individual. Teachers must ask themselves if the primary objective is to impress others with their knowledge or to communicate that knowledge.

While learning should encourage the development of language skills, the process must be done in a gradual manner. Teachers should begin discussions with words that secure the interest of the learner. Teachers can't afford to stumble with lots of hums, ah-ah, huh, or use words that are far above the comprehension of the learners. If teachers do not initially communicate with an understandable language, there may not be an opportunity for a second "hearing." Gradually, the spoken language can then be used to challenge the learner with increasing understanding.

Teachers must appreciate the power of words. Words can hurt and heal, open and close an audience, and discourage and encourage. Words have different meanings for different age groups and cultural groups. For example, even the basic meaning of being a Christian can vary. For some it may mean a faith relationship with Christ; for others it may simply mean going to church or doing good deeds. In foreign cultures being a Christian may mean being a westerner, an outsider; the word becomes a political description, instead of a spiritual one. Know the group and the individuals who make up the group. Then choose your words to meet the needs of your students.

Language is not limited to the spoken word. Body language communicates a stronger message than words. If there is disagreement between the spoken word and the body language, the body language is given more credibility or importance by the learner. It is hard to communicate interest if we fail to look at the person directly. How can the learner believe that we care if we won't look at him or her? The teacher cannot convince the learner that he is interested in the learner's ideas and feelings if the body stance does not communicate interest.

Body language that helps to communicate interest includes looking directly into the eyes of the speaker, maintaining an open body posture, slightly leaning forward, and respecting the body zone distance. Jesus said, "Let the little children come to me, and do not stop them; for it is to such as these that the kingdom of heaven belongs" (Matt. 19:14). No doubt in both His words and body gestures, Jesus showed His deep compassion for the little children. He not only had words that reached out to children but also arms that reached out to them. Like Jesus, teachers and learners should use language that facilitates total communication.

Sense Experience

How do we learn about the world? We learn through our senses; therefore, we must teach through our senses. Our senses are the vehicles through which we give, as well as receive communication with others. The more the senses are involved, the more channels we have to give and receive information. We are more likely to learn if we have opportunities to experience information with one or more of our senses.

Teaching should focus on varied sense experiences. Traditionally, teachers have appealed to an adult world primarily through aural experiences that focus exclusive attention on the lecture. How convincing is hearing alone? How often, after hearing a sermon, have you walked out of the church not being able to remember what you just heard? If we involve our sense of touch by writing or summarizing the main ideas expressed, we may remember and apply what we heard. The pastor or teacher may encourage greater learning if he can capture our different senses. If we can see it, touch it, hear it, and smell it, we're more apt to remember and apply it.

In the Lord's Supper, Jesus provided a truly varied learning experience for His followers, appealing to the disciples' various senses. Jesus spoke to them—hearing; He served them—touching; He gave them bread and wine—tasting and smelling; and He portrayed a selfless life before them—seeing. A total learning experience occurred for these disciples through the dramatic teachings of Jesus. The memory and practice of that Supper remained with the disciples.

Variety

Variety may or may not be the spice of life, but variety is definitely the spice of teaching. The only bad or ineffectual method is one that is constantly used. Our natural tendency is to use those methods which are most familiar or comfortable to us. However, we run the risk of boring ourselves, as well as our learners. Being somewhat unpredictable as a teacher encourages the learner to stay awake intellectually in the learning process. Keep them guessing, expecting, and exploring with their imagination.

Variety is one way to maintain attention and interest. Have you ever become bored with the subject that you are teaching? Does this boredom affect the presentation and the impact upon the learner? How predictable are your classes? Are there any surprises? Trying a different approach and presentation may rekindle your enthusiasm for the subject and your effectiveness in teaching. Jesus used variety as He taught others—questions and answers, parables, object lessons, field trips, large and small groups, and learning by doing. Learning with Jesus was anything but boring!

Relevancy/Application

Generally those who participate in Christian education do so voluntarily. We have few, if any, paid teachers. Those who come and participate do so freely. Parents may force their children to attend Sunday School and a college student may attend out of habit. In either case, the "coerced" or "habitual" student may not be ready to learn. One way of encouraging attendance and quality learning is emphasizing how the material affects, changes, and applies to daily life. Make it relevant; make it apply.

Our world is extremely pragmatic. We attend what we want to attend and learn what we want to learn. We participate in and learn what we believe will have some benefit for ourselves. Churches have more successful attendance if their learning opportunities appeal to genuine needs. For example, churches have little trouble attracting young married families if the church offers family educational opportunities. Churches promote quality Christian learning by showing how the biblical material is related to life needs, such as dealing with the marital partner, performing on the job, or handling stress on a daily basis. What we present in Christian learning must be relevant and applicable to the life concerns of people.

Demonstrating the value and application makes the material more alive and meaningful. Share your own experiences with the learner. Live the material in life and fall under the conviction of God's teaching. The effective teacher becomes a part of the learning process as an initiator and a fellow-participant. Provide concrete activities, as well as an opportunity for feedback and fellowship. The greater the opportunity to put the material into practice, the greater the opportunity for genuine growth and change.

To encourage relevancy we must ultimately believe in the value of what we teach and what we ask of the learner. We must be committed to the application and relevancy of the Christian faith. Jesus acknowledged His commitment: "For I have come down from heaven, not to do my own will, but the will of him who sent me" (John 6:38). Jesus was committed and still holds the keys to eternal life. Jesus said: "My sheep hear my voice. I know them, and they follow me. I give them eternal life, and they will never perish. No one will snatch them out of my hand " (John 10:27-28). Christian teaching/learning involves eternal life, both here and now and in the future.

Interest/Attention

While hitting a mule between the eyes may be one way of securing its attention, it can also lead to brain damage. Fortunately our learners are not mules; however, you must capture their attention. Without the focused or concentrated attention of the learner, little learning will occur.

Attention and interest go hand-in-hand. To what is initially interesting, we give our attention; to what we give our continued attention may become interesting to us. For example, I am interested in ways to improve my writing. Any program or person who offers such, immediately secures my attention. I pay close attention, especially if I am paying for the opportunity. Interest encourages my attentiveness.

Continued exposure to an idea may also make it eventually interesting and appealing. Fifteen years ago, I had no interest in computers and could envision little reason for a friend's taking a class in computers. That reveals quite a bit about my imagination and insight, doesn't it? Later, I saw advertisements, read material that showed what could be done with computers, and listened to the testimonies of my friends about the wonders of word processing. After my attention was secured through constant exposure, I was hooked. My interest followed attention. Now I cannot imagine writing anything without a computer with word processing capabilities. I am continuing to take classes in computer science which I thought useless fifteen years ago.

Teachers can work at securing the attention of their learners by constant exposure, as well as focusing on immediate learner interests. Secure interest and attention by the use of a new experience, the paradox, the question, the dramatic, the absurd, or the humorous. If you're discussing the missionary journeys of Paul, dress as Paul might have dressed. Have the learners close their eyes and imagine what it would be like to be in the temple when Jesus drove the moneychangers away. Ask questions to invoke interest such as what would have happened if _____? You fill in the blank. Securing attention and interest involves the use of our own creativity.

Catching the learner between the eyes involves being seen and being heard, but caution must be exercised. We must not dwell exclusively on the sensational. Christian teaching is not a three-ring circus or a carnival. However, good teaching is interesting because the teacher has devoted time and preparation to the process of teaching/learning. Interest and attention do not happen by mere accident. Work is involved.

Securing attention and interest must be viewed as a dynamic process, beginning with secured learner interest. Throughout the ebb and flow of the learning process, interest must be continually sustained. The end, as well as the middle, must be interesting and challenging, encouraging further learning. Always end the lesson with the learner yearning for a little bit more. Help the learner realize that learning is a lifelong process. The teacher must patiently remember that the interest and attention of the learner is dependent upon his or her maturity level. Jesus said, "I still have many things to say to you, but you cannot bear them now. When the Spirit of truth comes, he will guide you into all the truth; for he will not speak on his own, but will speak whatever he hears, and he will declare to you the things that are to come" (John 16:12-13). Chapter 5 will provide additional information on motivating and securing the interest of the learner in the pursuit of lifelong learning.

Modeling

One of my delights as a young boy was constructing model ships. I remember making replicas of the Nina, the Pinta, and the Santa Maria—Columbus' three ships on his maiden voyage to the New World. The models, in design and detail, were representative of a greater ship. Those ship models represented adventure, excitement, fortune, and freedom. As I grew older, I realized that models apply not only to ships, cars, and doll houses, but also to people. In fact, teachers were a powerful role model for me, even though I did not recognize it myself at the time.

Because the influence of the teacher is so persuasive, teachers must carefully model what they teach, especially in the Christian faith. No other factor can produce greater harm than an unworthy model; no factor can produce greater benefit than a worthy one. Individuals will emulate or follow the life demonstrated before them. Learners tend to live up to the standards and examples set before them. If little is expected and modeled, we tend to get little. If we expect a great deal and provide positive Christian modeling, we tend to get a great deal.

Various factors are involved in modeling. Human models should be real, worthy, and credible both in and out of the classroom. Christian modeling involves demonstrating the characteristics and life-style of Jesus Christ. Scripture records that God became flesh and dwelt among us. "And the Word became flesh and lived among us, and we have seen his glory as of a father's only son, full of grace and truth" (John 1:14). In a later chapter, we will focus upon selected characteristics of Jesus as the model teacher.

Competency

"I don't really know enough to teach the Bible. You need to get someone who knows more than I know." How often I have heard those comments from people who in fact knew enough to begin teaching. How many of us really ever know it all? Few, I think. This hesitancy to teach and to lead is not a new one. When confronted by God, Moses gave numerous excuses for his unworthiness (Ex. 4:11 ff). However,

God responded, "But I will be with your mouth and teach you what you are to speak" (Ex. 4:12). With God, Moses grew in both confidence and competency.

Teaching and learning involves a degree of competency; however, this competency does not mean that you must be an "expert" in everything. It does mean, however, working toward improving your competency and teaching abilities. Read books, attend seminars, associate with more experienced teachers, and attend training sessions. Competency is developed through the input of information, the practice of that information or skill, the reception of feedback, and continued practice. Developing competency is a continual process. No one ever arrives. If we think we have arrived at being the expert, we have actually fallen short of what we could be. The most competent are always learning.

Both the teacher and the learner must be given opportunity to improve and to develop their respective levels of competency. Strive not only for competency as teachers, but also for competency among our learners. The goal of teaching is to instruct another so that he in turn can become a teacher.

Teachers and learners must recognize that both successful experiences and failures can lead to competency. Failure at one lesson does not mean that success is impossible. Learning can occur from both our mistakes and our successes. Often we can learn much more from our failures than we do from our successes as evidenced in the relationship between Jesus and Peter.

Jesus gave Peter a great deal of responsibility in the new church. Matthew 16:18-19 states: "And I tell you, you are Peter, and on this rock I will build my church, and the gates of Hades will not prevail against it. I will give you the keys of the kingdom of heaven, and whatever you bind on earth will be bound in heaven, and whatever you loose on earth will be loosed in heaven."

Full of confidence, Peter would later say to Jesus, "Though all become deserters because of you, I will never desert you" (Matt. 26:33). After Jesus was betrayed by Judas, Peter would deny Jesus three times (Matt. 26:69-75). When Peter saw the risen Lord on the beach, "he put on some clothes, for he was naked, and jumped into the sea" (John 21:7). After Jesus fed the disciples a meal of fish, Jesus asked Peter three times if he loved Him. After each of Peter's affirmative answers, Jesus told Peter to "feed my sheep" (John 21:9-19). Rather than being forever defeated, Peter grew from his failure to become a great leader in the early church. This man of weakness and fear became a competent teacher and disciple through both success and failure.

Active Involvement

John Dewey, a great pragmatic educator of the nineteenth century, emphasized the learner's active involvement in learning. Simply stated, active involvement occurs when the learner has hands-on experiences. However, this idea was not new in the nineteenth century. In fact, the New Testament reveals learners who were actively involved in proclaiming and ministering the gospel. Jesus sent His disciples out to proclaim His kingdom and to work for the kingdom (Luke 10:1-12).

As a teacher, I learn from my students through their participation in learning. Actively involved students learn from each other. Active learning, which is contagious, involves the individual using his total self in the learning process.

Active learner involvement begins with learners selecting and formulating their own learning goals. The learning belongs to the learner. Let him have ownership and input. Give guidance as needed. Next, let the learner have input as you select the best teaching/learning strategy that will be used, such as lecture, discussion groups, research project, or drama. Ask the learner how he will know that learning has occurred. Use these responses to guide the activities and the evaluation. Active involvement should occur throughout the process from beginning to end as illustrated by the work of Jesus.

Just as He had actively involved the disciples in His earthly ministry, Jesus' last words to His disciples in Matthew 28:19-20 were words for active involvement; "Go therefore and make disciples of all nations, baptizing them in the name of the Father and of the Son and of the Holy Spirit, and teaching them to obey everything that I have commanded you. And remember, I am with you always, to the end of the age." Both the learner (the disciple) and the teacher (Jesus) were actively involved in the spread of the gospel. Later chapters will explore specific ways of involving the learner in his or her learning.

Environment

Environment is important to learning. A pleasant and well-resourced environment helps the teacher and learner function better. Learning environment involves two separate areas: the physical aspect of the environment and the spiritual climate.

The physical aspects appear first upon a casual glance into the room. Brightly colored pictures on the wall, well-organized resources around the room, comfortable temperature, and pleasant light add to the learning experience. However, we make a mistake if we wait for the newly equipped classroom to bring about great leaps of learning. Quality learning can occur in the most humble dwellings. Many great people of God have emerged from one-room churches and school houses.

While basic physical resources are significant, the second and more significant area of environment is the spiritual climate. A positive spiritual climate where God is honored contributes immeasurably to the learning process. Relationships are built among learners and between the teacher and learner. Additionally, the relationship of all participants to God is encouraged. Here learners are given the opportunity to try—both to succeed and to fail. An atmosphere that values the learning and seeks the excitement of new learning is a part of a positive spiritual climate. Believing in and relying upon the power of God to direct educational activities produces results. A positive spiritual climate enhances the experience for both teacher and learner.

Inadequate resources are minimized when the spiritual climate is positive. What happens around the event is often more powerful than the event itself. Proverbs 15:16-17 records: "Better is a little with the fear of the Lord than great treasure and trouble with it. Better is a dinner of vegetables where love is than a fatted ox and hatred with it." Rather than the contents of the meal, the more powerful and satisfying are the attitudes and relationships shared around the meal. Students will often forget the specifics of what they learned. However, they will not forget how they felt in the learning process. The attitudes and feelings experienced are powerful forces that influence future learning, attitude and behavior. The climate in Christian teaching and learning shapes the future of the learner.

Holy Spirit

The Holy Spirit is a vital part of the learning process in Christian education. In fact, genuine Christian education cannot exist apart from the work of the Holy Spirit. The Holy Spirit moves in the interactions between teacher and learner. The movement of the Holy Spirit takes place in various parts of life, such as in our conscious reflections (1 Cor. 2:10-11); in our minds (Rom. 7:14-25); and in our motivations (Rom. 8; 1 Cor. 12—14).

The Holy Spirit provides gifts for the upbuilding of the body of Christ. Christian teaching and learning are a part of the continual upbuilding of the body of Christ (the church). The Holy Spirit allows the individuals to share in self-sacrificing or agape love. Agape love transforms both learner and teacher. The yielding of the learner and teacher to the work of the Holy Spirit keeps the learning alive and meaningful. Jesus said the Comforter (Holy Spirit) would come among us to do great and mighty acts. This same spirit makes Christian learning and teaching distinctive from other types of learning.

Looking Back

Now you have completed the second major step in obtaining your passport to the world of Christian teaching and learning—a theory of teaching/learning. Remember that the theory you use must be your own. This chapter has shared with you the following skeletal outline of a theory: relationship, feedback, understandable language, sense experience, variety, relevancy/application, interest/attention, modeling, competency, active involvement, environment, and the Holy Spirit. As a responsible teacher, you must develop these ideas for yourself. These ideas will form the basic framework for your teaching. You may add additional elements, and you may minimize other elements. Like a seasoned traveler, a seasoned teacher knows what works best in each situation.

Looking Ahead

The next step in obtaining your passport will be reviewing the role of the learner. Remember the learner is the focus of our attention as teachers.

Learning Activities

1. "The Importance of Having a Theory"
   A. Create a diagram to illustrate the relationship between theory and practice.
   B. What importance, if any, does a theory of learning have to a practice of teaching? Explain.
2. "Relationships"
   A. Describe the most important relationship that you have ever experienced. What were the characteristics of that relation-

ship? What made that relationship significant? What was necessary for maintaining that relationship?

B. What was the most meaningful teaching relationship that you have ever experienced? What were the characteristics of that relationship?

3. "Better to Give Than To Receive—But Not In Feedback"

A. Think about yesterday. On a sheet of paper divided into two sections, list feedback that you gave other people. On the opposite side, list feedback that you received from other people. Under each feedback item listed, write the consequence of each feedback item.

B. "A day without feedback is a day without sunshine." Explain your reactions to the above statement.

4. "Mankind—the Language Machine"

A. What different audiences do you communicate with during the day? Do you use a different language or choose different words to communicate to these groups? If so, why? What would happen if you changed how you communicated to each group?

B. What is the relationship between body language and spoken language? What happens if these two languages do not match?

5. "Making Sense of the Experience"

A. In the various activities of church, what senses are used? Can you think of ways that the use of the various senses would improve the activities of church? Why or why not? Explain.

B. What sense experiences do you provide for learners? Think of ways that you might improve your instruction by appealing to more senses. Explain

6. "A Variety Pack of Teaching/Learning"

A. List as many different teaching methods as you can. List the strengths and weaknesses of each.

B. Think of an especially "great" teacher that you had. What methods did this teacher use?

C. Think of an especially "poor" teacher that you had. What methods did this teacher use?

7. "How Does This Apply?"

A. Draw a picture that represents ways in which the learning process should be relevant to the learner.

B. Make an acrostic with the word "Relevancy" or "Application." List words, phrases or sentences that will increase the likelihood of making learning relevant.

8. "Securing Attention or Interest"

If you are a teacher, analyze your own teaching style. List things that you do that encourage interest, as well as things that discourage interest.

9. "Making Models"

A. Name a significant human model for you. What are his or her qualities? What impact, if any, would there be if the model "failed" you in some way?

B. Name someone for whom you are a model. How does being a model make you feel. What can you do to improve your being a model for someone else?

10. "Competency"

A. Describe, in your own words, what is a competent teacher and a competent learner. Explain.

B. What would increase your competencies as both teacher and learner? How can you go about acquiring those competencies? Be specific.

11. "Keep 'em Active"

A. Divide a sheet of paper in half. On one side write "Passive Learning"; on the other side write "Active Learning." Write down the advantages and disadvantages of each type of learning.

B. Think of a lesson that you recently taught or a lesson in which you were the student. Redesign the lesson to encourage more learner activity.

12. "Looking at the Environment"

A. Compare and contrast the spirit in a good learning situation with that of a poor learning situation.

B. Create a mural in which you depict the essential spiritual elements in a good learning situation.

13. "The Holy Spirit"

A. Identify ways that the Holy Spirit works in the lives of learners.

B. Identify ways that the Holy Spirit has helped you in either teaching, learning, or both. Share this information with a friend.

C. List ways that you could become more dependent upon the Holy Spirit in both teaching and learning.

3. | The Learner

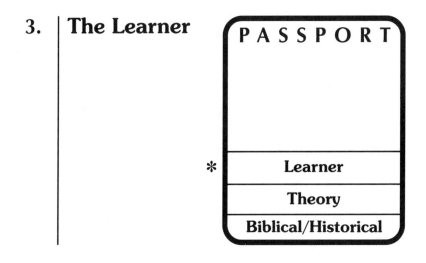

PASSPORT

* | **Learner**

Theory

Biblical/Historical

Establishing Importance

"I teach the Bible," one teacher responded proudly. Another teacher admitted, "Well, I teach people. The Bible does not need to be taught anything; however, people do need to be taught." While both views represent differences of opinion on the surface, most Christian teachers would recognize the importance of both the learner and the curriculum material. This chapter will take the perspective of the learner. We are in the business of teaching people and helping them learn. To teach people, we must know people. To teach people, we must learn about people.

Defining Chapter Goals

Now we shall study the learner as we apply for the passport to teaching/learning. In examining the recipient of our teaching, the learner, we must first discover all that we can about the person. We will briefly examine the biblical and theological information regarding the learner; then, we will examine additional dimensions of the learner's development, such as cognitive development, social and emotional development, moral development, physical development, and spiritual needs. At the end of this chapter, you should be able to do the following:

- describe key biblical concepts of human beings and their implications for teaching/learning;
- identify cognitive implications for teaching in various age groups;
- discuss the implications of the social and emotional development to the teaching/learning process;
- discuss the importance of moral development and reasoning ability to Christian education;
- describe the relationship between physical needs and learning; and
- discuss what is meant by describing life as a journey of faith and its implications for teachers.

Biblical Understanding

A biblical understanding of mankind is worthy of a volume within itself. Space does not permit an exhaustive discussion of this important area. However, several key ideas will be explored about humankind's nature that have significance in Christian teaching/learning.

Dust of the Ground (Gen. 2:7)

Two aspects of human creation must be kept in balance: "dust of the ground" and "image of God." In Genesis 2:7, we discover that Adam was created from the "dust of the ground." The "dust of ground" provides a clear illustration that mankind is a part of the created order, just as the other handiworks of God's creation. Consequently, humans have characteristics common with other animals. Principles that govern the life of animals also govern the life of people. For example, both humans and animals share similar needs: shelter, food, and water. We can understand a part of human nature by scientific inquiry.

As teachers we must be open to two sets of information about our learner—the biblical and the scientific. Because people are created from the dust, we can gain information about them as we study such disciplines as biology, physiology, anatomy, psychology, and sociology. However, science alone does not give us a full picture of the learner. We must examine the spiritual side (image of God). To teach people we must understand them both theologically and scientifically.

Image of God (Gen. 1:27)

This aspect involves mankind's being created in the "image of God." Impossible to describe fully, the "image of God" has far-reaching consequences for understanding people. The image of God may involve humans being created for relationship and fellowship because of the very nature of a relational God. Genesis 3:8 shows how God fellowshiped with Adam and Eve. Out of this fellowship with God, humans have the capacity for fellowship with themselves, others, and the natural world. Being human involves having significant fellowship needs.

While we are human from birth, there is a sense in which we learn to be human through contacts with other people. Individuals reared in isolation, deprived of human fellowship and nurture, develop into something less than human. Children reared in isolation are often animal-like in their behavior. Deprived of human contact, these "wolf" children do not possess the needed social skills. In His infinite wisdom, God created this need for fellowship and through ultimate fellowship with God and with others, persons have the possibility for achieving their potential.

Involved in the "image of God" is mankind's ability to reason. More than any other creature, humans have the ability to approach and attempt to grasp the nature of his Creator. Mankind's capacity for great intellect may be developed either for good or for evil. In addition, as a result of the ability to reason, mankind has a unique ability to communicate. A part of human nature involves the need to communicate with the Divine and with others. Communication allows for both the expression and growth of relationships.

Teachers must acknowledge the implications of the "image of God" as they plan for teaching/learning activities. Learners need to be involved in relationships with others as they seek to grow with and from others. Humans have a capacity to reason that must be developed and nurtured. Men and women are not merely machines but have potential for creative thought and activity. Good teaching utilizes their cognitive potential. Additionally, human beings have both the need and the potential to communicate. Like the above characteristics, teachers should develop the learner's ability to communicate with self, others, and God. Knowing human capacity and uniqueness provides guidelines for aims in teaching and learning.

Sin and rebellion (Gen. 3:1-24)

While the more positive aspects of human nature have been highlighted, the Christian view of teaching and learning demands that a serious examination of sin be attempted. Through an act of disobedience people have sinned, and therefore robbed themselves of fellowship with God. Deuteronomy 5:7 states: "You shall have no other gods before me." Through our disobedience, we attempt to become our own god.

The cycle of mankind's disobedience to God has been repeated in each generation and in each individual life. Each individual has personally sinned and is in need of personal redemption through Christ. We live also in a sinful world where the consequences of past sins abound. These sinful patterns established in the world influence mankind toward personal acts of sin.

Sin may be described in many ways. Popularly, we think of sin as a list of bad things we do. Although sin is definitely bad, this view may not provide a complete understanding of sin. According to Scripture, sin is missing the mark or failing to live up to God's expectations for us. Not only is sin bad, but it prevents our having a quality life. Regardless of our personal life-style, Scripture teaches that we all have sinned (Rom. 3:23). While some learners lead upright lives, they are nevertheless in need of personal redemption and the restoration of their relationship with God.

As Christian teaching/learning brings the learner's life into harmony with God, other changes will also take place. For example, new attitudes and behaviors emerge as we become rightly related to God through faith. Some changes will occur abruptly and dramatically; other changes are more gradual and subtle. Let us lead the learner to self-discovery. Changes by choice and personal conviction are more powerful than changes by coercion.

The teacher must provide for a learning process that acknowledges both the good and the evil of people. Mankind's ability to reason, the gift of stewardship (see Gen. 2:19-20; 1:26), the need for meaningful work (Gen. 2:15) and the need for creativity (Gen. 1:28) should be part of the learning process across the life span. Christian teaching/learning must equally assist persons in acknowledging sin and in moving to closer fellowship with God.

Cognitive Development

Each learner differs in cognitive or intellectual development and must be understood in light of this individuality. General statements about certain age groups must also be considered in light of individuals who may vary somewhat from the average. Teachers must teach in light of the learner's mental abilities. Various researchers have contributed to our understanding of the cognitive growth of the individual. Piaget, one of the most influential psychologists in the twentieth century, summa-rizes these age groups.[1] The following description is an adaptation of Piaget's findings on the intellectual growth of the learner. Along with the descriptions are brief ways this knowledge can be used in teaching.

Infant (0-2 years)

One of the major intellectual goals for the infant is mastery of the relationship between his senses and his motor skills. The young child is beginning to develop a sense of self as distinct from the environment. By the end of the first two years of life, the young child can do such things as having goal-directed behavior (he goes to another room to get a favorite toy); knowing characteristics of familiar objects (he can know his church and the location of his Sunday School class); using more complex language (he can sing songs he learns in church and join in short prayers); and acquiring object permanence (objects continue to exist when out of the individual's field of vision such as when Dad leaves him for "Big Church"). These accomplishments form the basis for future cognitive growth and development.

Younger child (2-7 years)

At this stage, the child is egocentric and thinks all events center around her and her intents. This egocentrism has various implications. If the parents divorce, the child considers herself responsible. The world revolves around self. She lives in a world of magic, where reality and fantasy closely intermingle. The child believes that mere wishes can alter reality, such as causing the sun to shine by wishing the rain away. Inanimate objects have life and breath to this child. When she is sick, her favorite stuffed animal is also sick. Although the child is quickly developing language and communication skills, the child is quite literal in thinking and comprehension.

These mental characteristics have direct bearing upon the teaching/learning situation. Teachers must be aware of the sensitive nature of the child. The child regards everything very personally. If someone fails to greet him, he takes it personally. If he gives the wrong answer to a Bible question, he takes the mistake personally. Positive correction that builds up the confidence of the child is essential. Another example is family problems which the child personalizes beyond his level of responsibility. Teachers may help children who suffer anguish and guilt by listening to them, by encouraging them, and by being available for support.

Another significant implication for teaching is the literal thinking of the child. We must teach carefully because much of our religious language tends to be symbolic. Children at this age are not capable of understanding symbolism. They take things quite literally. Carefully chosen words and careful explanations are important in teaching this age group.

Older child (7-11 years)

This age is marked by the development of more complex mental skills. This child is acquiring the concepts of conservation (amounts remain the same regardless of changes in shape) such as number, substance, length, area, weight, and volume. Now the learner is aware of the viewpoint of others. With improved short- and long-term memory, he or she can deal simultaneously with several aspects of a situation or an object. Although problem-solving abilities exist, concrete examples are necessary. Toward the end of this age, the child grasps the nature of symbols and symbolic language. Thus, he will be able to work in the future with more abstract issues, such as mathematics, theology, literature, and the sciences.

Teaching this age group can be more adventurous with the child's new cognitive abilities. However, teachers must remember that each child differs in these abilities. No two children are alike. Toward the end of this period, the child has the capacity for more understandable Bible memory and application. Case studies are appropriate as ways to encourage thinking in Bible-related materials. Keep in mind that the thinking is still concrete for most children.

Adolescent (12 plus years)

Gradually, the adolescent develops the ability to think and reason like a scientist. The adolescent can observe facts; take the viewpoint of others; formulate hypotheses; test the hypotheses; and revise thinking if needed. The young male or female is beginning to formulate his or her own views of the world and to test these newly acquired beliefs.

The individual at this stage of development is inclined to be idealistic. As a result, both young males and females are apt to become disappointed with the world. Much of everyday life is spent in wishful speculation. Adolescents daydream and speculate on philosophical and political issues. Preoccupied with self, the adolescent believes that no one has ever felt or loved as he or she loves and that everyone is watching him or her. Constantly searching for something noble with which to identify, they become vulnerable. For example, adolescents are a good target for religious cults that offer acceptance and something in which to believe.

Youth need teachers who are sensitive to their quickly developing cognitive abilities. Activities must be designed that foster and encourage these abilities. If not, youth may decide that religious teachings are insignificant, otherwise they would be more intellectually challenged. Youth teachers must challenge them intellectually, as well as spiritually.

Adult (young adult onward)

Generally, the adult's thinking turns from the philosophical to the pragmatic. Less idealistic, the person is more concerned with the daily issues of living, such as food, clothing, shelter, and transportation. Adults no longer have the luxury of being sheltered from the world in order to speculate. Thinking develops around the issues of making a living. Increasingly, the intellectual processes are directed toward more focused and more practical concerns of life and work.

As the individual becomes older, intellectual abilities gradually change. In late adulthood, the speed of processing information declines, and the individual may take longer to respond. The adult is more apt to learn new material if it is relevant to his life needs and interests. Various memory devices may improve his memory for new materials. Strategies for storing and organizing the information are helpful. Although intellectual changes occur, learning is still possible.

Those responsible for adult teaching/learning activities have great influence in shaping the Christian faith of the adults. In adulthood, faith often becomes real for the first time. Adults want information and answers that will make a difference in their everyday lives. Practicality is a key issue. Like other age groups, personalized teaching/learning is critical.

As teaching strategies, styles, and methodologies are developed, the cognitive level of the learner must be taken into account. Each age group has its own characteristics and implications for teaching. As you communicate with learners, consider their capacities to understand. Our presentations must not be too far above or too far below the learner's own current abilities. Otherwise, the teaching is less than effectual. This idea will be explored in chapter 7 with additional teaching implications for each age group.

Social and Emotional Development

As social creatures, human beings are created for relationships. These relationships may be healthy or unhealthy; constructive or destructive; inclusive or exclusive. To teach more effectively, we must understand the learner's social and emotional needs. Social and emotional needs are integrally related. Twentieth-century psychologist Erik Erikson has provided valuable information to understanding both the social and psychological needs of mankind.[2] The following age-level survey is based upon insights from Erikson.

The young child is born into the world totally helpless, depending upon others for his own physical and emotional well-being. With the proper fulfillment of these needs, the young child begins to develop a close attachment with another significant individual. Out of this attachment, or bonding, the child begins to develop his own sense of security and trust with the world.

This initial relationship and its consequences form the basis for all future relationships. Poor attachment early in life may predispose one to poor relationships in the future. For example, poorly attached children often have difficulty in forming healthy relationships and in developing a positive self-image. Healthy relationships provide the encouragement, trust, and energy to grow beyond ourselves. Rather than being inwardly directed, healthy relationships stimulate exploration of the world, mastery of life's tasks, and establishment of other relationships.

From infancy, the human being sets upon a quest of future relationships. The quality of these relationships depends upon the individual's own self-concept and the perceived sense of worth from the evaluation of others. Many lifelong skills are developed during the early school years: sharing; communication; learning rules; being a team player; self-sufficiency skills; and academic skills of reading, writing, and arithmetic. Failures or successes at these skills influence how he feels about himself and how he responds in society.

In adolescence, the challenge is to determine his or her own identity and destiny with the greater world. These new mental abilities and physical changes (puberty) create a disequilibrium (unbalance) or tension for the learner. The struggling adolescent must deal with issues of sexuality and vocational identity. How he or she "fits" into the ongoing panorama of history and the human race becomes important. Once this identity is formed, the individual is then free to make mature commitments to significant love relationships.

The adult increasingly learns how to invest in lasting relationships. While the norm may be a long-term relationship culminating in marriage, other types of relationships are possible. The individual may choose to devote his life in service to others as the apostle Paul did. However, the mature individual, who was created for relationship, must now determine, in a more constructive fashion, his or her own contributions to the growth and life of others.

Throughout life, there are periods of review and self-examination. Typically, the individual questions involvement with self and others. Take the example of Bob and Helen, both approaching fifty. When they married, their dream was to work hard and retire early to enjoy those years. Bob was to paint, and Helen was to open an antique shop. Both wanted the freedom to go on short mission trips. Twenty-five years later, they have no retirement plan. Bob realizes that it is too late to make a vocational move. Companies are looking for younger men. The man who would have been a great painter has not picked up a paint brush in years, except to paint the interior of his heavily mortgaged house. Helen has devoted the last twenty-five years to her children and now stares at television for hours at a time since the last child has left for college. It seems as though the children only write to ask for money.

Middle-aged adults, like Bob and Helen, often face such social and emotional crises when realizing that certain ambitions will go unfulfilled; acknowledging that one's life may be half over; accepting that children have left home; and making adjustments that accompany decreased physical health. The quality of life is often measured by how basic relationships have been formed and nurtured. Emotional pleasure is often measured by the quality of these various investments in relationships.

If teachers ignore the tremendous social/emotional needs and contributions of the learner, the learner is robbed of an important element of humanity. Social and emotional needs are a part of a holistic view of the learner. Teaching/learning must seek to nurture and complement these basic needs. Ideas such as trust, security, attachment, and relationships are basic to teaching/learning. These types of needs can only be met through the involvement of caring teachers and fellow learners. Otherwise, humans are treated as little more than machines.

Moral Development

Moral development deals with choices and decisions we make. It is an important element because Christian teaching/learning involves how we feel, think, and act in moral issues. As we mature, our moral reasoning changes. Two researchers in the area of moral development are Piaget and Kohlberg.

Piaget uses the term *heteronomous morality* to describe the moral thinking of the child from four to seven years. This child thinks that rightness or goodness is based upon the consequences of the behavior. For example, if Anne steals a cookie and isn't caught, the act is good or right. If Anne is caught, the act is wrong or bad. Rules are seen as all powerful and unchangeable. If a teacher or preacher says it is right, it must be right because these people are all powerful. These children also believe that punishment will occur immediately. If Johnny does something wrong, he will immediately pay the consequences. These characteristics form the basis for their moral reasoning and choices.

Piaget calls the reasoning of children ten years and older *autonomous morality*. These children consider the intention of the person, not just the behavior. If Amy breaks the jar while trying to help Mommy, the act is good or right. If Amy breaks the jar while disobeying Mommy, the act is bad or wrong. Rules are seen as subject to change and sometimes punishment can be avoided. Moral autonomists consider the situation and the individual in moral choices and decisions.[3]

Kohlberg builds on Piaget's findings and describes three levels of moral reasoning. The first is the preconventional level where we make decisions based upon either being punished or being rewarded. Harriet acts good because she either wants a reward or does not want to be punished. The second level is the conventional level in which we make decisions based upon the rules of society. Andy wants to be a good member of society so he follows the rules of the group. The third level is the postconventional level in which the individual makes decisions based upon his or her own beliefs that go beyond mere societal expectations. These beliefs may be religious, such as obeying the Golden Rule.[4]

Christian teachers should be sensitive to the moral reasoning of their learners. Do your learners make decisions based upon fear of being caught? Are they afraid God will send a bolt of lighting to "zap'em" if they misbehave? If so, their faith may be based more on fear than trust and love. Do your learners make decisions in order to be accepted by the crowd? Peer pressure is a real threat to any age.

As learners develop in their ability to make decisions, challenge them to respond in ways pleasing to God based on obedience, love, and trust. Show what the Bible has to say about choices they will encounter.

Share your own experiences with decision making. Don't become discouraged if your learners are less mature than you want them to be. Accept them and work with them in helping them to mature. No one is born fully mature; maturity takes time and experience. Stay with them, assisting them on their journey.[5]

Physical Development

Teachers must recognize that the physical aspects of the learner are a crucial part of the learning process. We teach individuals who are physical, as well as intellectual, spiritual, and social/emotional. Physical needs are related to higher needs, including our need to learn. If physical needs are not being met, other needs may not be met or satisfied. When Elijah was discouraged and depressed, God ministered to him through rest and nutrition (1 Kings 19:4-6). It is difficult to focus on higher pursuits if there is a health problem or a nutritional deficiency. Concern for learning also means concern for the learner's physical needs.

Abraham Maslow, another noted twentieth-century American psychologist, did not deal directly with physical development; however, his research has implications for the role of physical needs in motivating behavior.

According to Maslow, we are motivated in light of our need. For example, if some needs are not being met, we engage in various behaviors to meet or reduce those deficits. Maslow's hierarchy begins with our lower level needs and moves upward. These needs involve our physiological needs; safety needs; love and belonging needs; esteem needs; self-actualization; and the need to know. Before higher level needs can be met, these lower level needs must be satisfied.

Our behavior often depends upon this hierarchy. As situations change, so does our motivations and behavior. The college freshman provides insight into how this hierarchy operates. The typical high school student has had his physiological needs, his safety needs, his love and belonging needs, and self-esteem needs met. Rising through the ranks as a high school senior, he is somewhat secure with the routines and structures of daily life. He or she has learned the basics.

As a college freshman, behaviors are now focused upon meeting previously met basic needs. Early pursuits include discovering the hours of the cafeteria and local fast food establishments. Each day the freshman goes to his mail box in the hopes of receiving word from some close friend back home or at another university. The first weeks and even years of college are devoted to establishing meaningful friendships. Academically, the last two years are generally more productive than the first two. This new improvement in academic performance, in part, shows that he has settled down into the college routine. Having had his basic needs met, he is once more able to concentrate on higher needs.

Teachers in a college Sunday School department can use Maslow's ideas in reaching and teaching their students. Let the college department be a place of safety, a place where they belong. Regardless of how bad the week has been, let the college students find a haven in Sunday School in which they can feel good. Provide opportunities for fellowships that include meals. Home cooked food means a great deal to those whose main diet is cafeteria food. On special occasions, send cards, snacks, small gifts, and notes to remind them of your concern for their well-being. Encourage them to establish relationships with one another and develop their own support teams that can help meet the challenges of campus life. As these types of needs are met, challenge them to learn more and more of the Christian faith and how it applies to their academic studies. Relate what they study in the university to what they study in Sunday School. Let them respond and share their ideas, feelings, and questions.

The above discussion has dealt with physical needs in very general terms that relate to learning. Having physical needs met can increase the likelihood of learning occurring. Otherwise, unmet physical needs can deter learning. To be concerned with the higher needs of the learner, we must not overlook these lower needs related to mere survival.

Looking Back

In this discussion of the learner, the idea of relationships has been explored in various contexts. The learner who is relational by nature is on a spiritual journey of relationships. Just as people are physical beings, people are by nature spiritual beings. Mankind has an inherent need for relationship or orientation toward something greater than self. In a sense, the quest or search for relationship is spiritual. Each person chooses the relationships to be pursued. The relationship may be with God, other people, physical pleasures, money, power, or prestige. We each have a void that we wish to fill.

The need to have something to which his or her whole life can be directed is basic to each person. Each of us searches for some meaning in life. We may term this humanity's faith development. Each person develops some type of faith orientation which may or may not be toward the Christian faith. It may be toward a materialistic orientation, a sexual orientation, or a power orientation.

Men and women spend their lives searching for the restored garden of Eden where perfect communion with the Creator existed. Not all searches and explorations are healthy and constructive. Ultimately, some searches and conclusions are destructive. Some searches end in meaningless materialism, drug or alcohol abuse, sexual immorality, empty religion, and death. Jesus points us in the proper direction when He said, "I am the way, and the truth, and the life. No one comes to the Father except through me" (John 14:6).

The teacher must be aware of mankind's need for spiritual restoration. Mankind has always had a need for commitment, for worship, and for participation with the Divine in a holy mission. God gave His Chosen People the privilege of being a priestly nation to other nations (Ex. 19:6). Had the role and responsibilities been taken seriously, many problems would have been avoided and benefits would have been reaped.

The journey of faith begins with conception and culminates with death. Throughout the journey, there are various tasks which each individual must face. Religious developmental tasks are dependent, in part, upon the maturity of the individual and teachings of the church. Religious tasks common to most age groups would include conversion, worship, church membership, knowledge and convictions, attitudes, and growth in Christian living and Christian service.[6] Dependent upon the maturity levels of the individual learner, these basic tasks find their own unique expression. Children need worship services just as adults, but the specific expressions (length, participation, music, message, etc.) of that need would differ. Each age finds its own religious developmental tasks to fulfill.

The sensitive Christian teacher regards faith as a journey. Each teacher, from the nursery to the senior adult class, is part of the terrain for those on a spiritual journey. It is our responsibility to find the best way to minister to the learner. We must provide nourishment, guidance, encouragement, and instruction to the pilgrim (learner) as he travels. In the journey, our learners eventually become teachers as they help others in their spiritual pilgrimage. The journey's end is to be conformed to the image of Christ (Rom. 8:29).

Bruce Powers in his book *Faith Development* provides a good illustration of faith development. He states:

Faith development cannot be divided into compartments. Rather it can be likened to the growth of a plant: seed, root, stem, leaf, bud, bloom. Each step happens in sequence, yet all are dependent on the earlier and continuing phases. All phases are the plant; the bloom is no more the plant than are the leaves or roots. So it is with faith; all phases are faith. Yet there is a distinct pattern of development.[7]

Jesus said that some would sow and some would reap (John 4:37). Regardless of where we are in the process with our learners and regardless of where our learners are in the process of faith, we contribute significantly to that ongoing growth. In order to nurture the faith, we must know the learner. The more we know and the more we apply, the more we can encourage new life to begin and to multiply. Faith is both caught and taught by our example.

The third component of your passport has been completed—the learner. To know fully the learner is an impossibility, but each teacher must try his or her best. The more we know those whom we teach, the more effective teachers we can become. Each learner has spiritual, cognitive, emotional, social, and physical needs. Each of these needs, in turn, influences his own learning and, in turn, our own teaching.

Looking Ahead

Now we turn to the fourth element in applying for your passport to teaching—the teacher. Pay close attention to the next chapter as we look at the Model Teacher and you. By looking at the characteristics of Jesus Christ, you may discover characteristics that will improve your life both as learner and as teacher.

Notes

1. Refer to the works of Piaget which include: *The Language and Thought of the Child; The Moral Judgment of the Child;* and *The Origins of Intelligence in Children.*

2. Refer to works of Erickson which include: *Childhood and Society; Insight and Responsibility; Identity, Youth, and Crisis; Dimensions of a New Identity; Life History and the Historical Moment;* and *The Life Cycle Completed: A Review.*

3. John W. Santrock, *Life Span Development,* 3d ed. (Dubuque, Iowa: Wm. C. Brown Co., Publishers, 1989), 275-76.

4. See Lawrence Kohlberg, *Essays on Moral Development, Volume I: The Philosophy of Moral Development: Moral Stages and the Idea of Justice,* and

Volume II: The Psychology of Moral Development: The Nature and Validity of Moral Stages.

5. For further study see Donald M. Joy, ed., *Moral Development Foundations: Judeo-Christian Alternatives to Piaget/Kohlberg.*
6. Charles A. Tidwell, *Educational Ministry of the Church* (Nashville: Broadman, 1982), 64-65.
7. Bruce P. Powers, *Growing Faith* (Nashville: Broadman, 1982), 21.

Learner Assessment Profile

1. Cognitive Development: Focus upon the current cognitive level and abilities of the learner as a group and as an individual.
    Observations: Implications:

2. Physical Development: Focus upon the current physical development level and abilities of the learner as a group and as an individual.
    Observations: Implications:

3. Spiritual Development: Focus upon the current spiritual development level and abilities of the learner as a group and as an individual.
    Observations: Implications:

4. Social and Emotional Development: Focus upon the current social and emotional developmental level and abilities of the learner as a group and as an individual.
    Observations: Implications:

5. Moral Development: Focus upon the current moral developmental level and abilities of the learner as a group and as an individual.
    Observations: Implications:

6. Special Needs and Circumstances: Focus upon the current special needs of the learner as a group and as an individual.
    Observations: Implications:

Learning Activities

1. Biblical Understanding of Man
    A. Read Genesis 1—11. List as many facts about mankind's

creation and subsequent life as recorded in the Genesis account. Beside each of these facts list the implications that each fact has for daily life.

B. Express in your own words the meaning of the following phrases: "dust of the earth"; "image of God"; and "sin."

C. What is the importance, if any, of having a biblical view of human beings? Discuss.

D. What role does a biblical understanding of mankind have for Christian teaching/learning?

2. Cognitive Development

A. Visit different ages in your Sunday School. As you observe in the various classes, watch for the evidences of the cognitive (intellectual) level of the learners. Make a list of their common characteristics. List ways that the teacher utilizes these characteristics in their teaching. Can you think of ways of how the teaching might be improved? Explain.

B. How do you believe that an individual teacher can cope in his teaching with individual cognitive differences?

C. Now you have a brief understanding of the cognitive abilities of the young child (2-7 years). What are the implications, if any, for presenting the gospel to this child?

D. Create a series of pictures that represent how the individual changes in his cognitive abilities. Each picture should depict a cognitive ability of a different age groups. Placed side by side, these pictures form a mural of the cognitive growth of the individual.

3. Social and Emotional Development

A. What are the relationships between social and emotional development? Reflect upon your own personal experiences and that of others. Use these examples as you describe the relationship.

B. What is the relationship between early bonding (attachment) and later relationships? Explain.

C. Learners often act in a group learning situation in the same manner as they do in their family. React to the above statement.

D. Identify ways that you can provide for the social needs of learners.

E. Identify ways that you can provide for the emotional enrichment of learners.

4. Moral Development

A. Describe how you reason (decide) about your own moral choices. Be as specific as you can.

B. If you teach a group, describe how the group generally goes about making a moral choice.

C. What influences contribute to positive moral decision making? Give examples.

5. Physical Development

A. Based on your own experience, how do physical factors influence learning?

B. What ways, if any, can a teacher adapt the teaching/ learning process to the physical needs of the learner? Be specific.

C. Create an analogy to describe the relationship between physical development and learning.

6. Journey of Faith

A. Faith may be described as a journey. Describe what is meant by that statement.

B. Create a short story that depicts the development of faith.

C. Describe what you consider the key elements in faith development.

4. | The Teacher

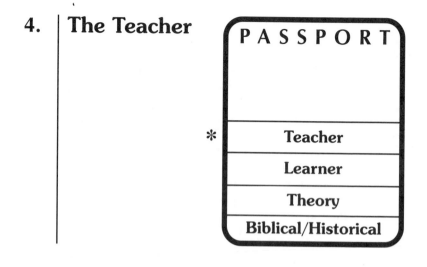

PASSPORT

*

Teacher
Learner
Theory
Biblical/Historical

Establishing Importance

"Tomorrow, I will share with you the three most important elements in teaching," challenged the educational psychology professor. The next morning she said, "Empathy, trustworthiness, and congruence. These are the most significant elements in the teaching process." Later, I would learn that my professor was emphasizing elements derived from the work of Carl Rogers, noted American psychologist and counselor. With increased study and years of practical teaching experience, I came to realize the truth of her initial response. The personality or the characteristics of the teacher are crucial.

Think about a subject that sends cold chills down your spine. Perhaps it is math, science, or English. Having taught statistics for several years, I discovered that a few of my students had an intense fear of math. A part of my teaching involved convincing them that they could do the work. As I questioned my students, I discovered they often associated the subject they hated with a particular dreaded teacher. Somehow the negative experience with the teacher influenced their fear for the subject. While they have long left that teacher behind, the teacher's influence still remains in regard to their perceived ability to learn various subject matters.

On the other hand, I have had students who first became interested in a subject because of the influence of a particular teacher. Again the teacher's personality influenced their attitude toward learning. The teacher's influence makes a difference. No one element will more quickly make or break the teaching/learning process than the personality of the teacher.

Defining Chapter Goals

The fourth part of obtaining your passport to teaching/learning is investigating the teacher, especially the teacher's personality. This chapter will integrate the research of Abraham Maslow, the teaching characteristics of Jesus, and implications for teaching. At the conclusion of this chapter, the reader should be able to do the following:

- explain the importance of the teacher's personality to the teaching/learning process;
- identify selected characteristics found in Maslow's research into self-actualizers;
- relate these characteristics to the life of Jesus; and
- summarize ways to develop these characteristics in your own life.

Teaching Personality

From ancient to modern times, people have debated the role of heredity and environment in shaping personality. Are we born with certain personality traits? Does environment determine our specific personality characteristics? Ancient Greek philosopher Aristotle argued that heredity was the more important personality agent; his student, Plato, argued that environment was the important personality agent. The ancient debate continues.

Modern theorists in personality research found that newborns differ in the following dimensions: activity level, adaptability, rhythmicity, approach-withdrawal, sensory threshold, predominant mood quality, mood expression intensity, distractibility, and attention span/persistence.[1] Arnold Buss and Robert Plomin believe that individuals differ in the following three dimensions of personality: sociability, emotionality, and excitability.[2] A growing number of researchers believe that individuals are born with a stable set of characteristics that are modifiable by later experiences. While heredity is a strong influence on personality, the strength of the relationships generally declines following infancy into childhood and adolescence. As a teacher and counselor, I believe that personality traits are influenced not only by heredity, but also by conscious choice and environmental influence.

Whatever the sources of these personality traits, they are highly influential in terms of impact upon other people, especially in teaching. As people of authority, teachers serve as powerful role models for their learners. Teachers have the power to guide, to shape, and to influence human destiny. What traits are influential in teaching? The work of Abraham Maslow may provide insight into identifying key personality traits significant in teachers.

Maslow studied individuals whom he considered to be self-actualizers, individuals described as striving to reach their potential. Within these selected individuals, Maslow identified fifteen positive characteristics.[3] Self-actualizers are more prone to influence others to self-actualize because of the life-style they model. These characteristics have been modified in light of their appropriateness to the Christian teaching/ learning process. Each of these traits will be examined in light of the model teacher—Jesus Christ. Finally, specific guidelines will be provided to encourage development of these traits.

Clear Vision of Reality

College teachers, even those in church-related institutions, have often been accused of living in ivy-covered towers with little contact with the harsh realities of life. Because of this devotion to the ideal, teachers have been accused of being unrealistic and impractical. However, teachers are equippers of students who live in the world. Teachers must not only strive for the ideal but also acknowledge the realities of life. Clarity of vision is essential.

Teachers should possess the ability to see life clearly in light of strengths and weaknesses, possibilities and probabilities, beauty and ugliness, and as it is and as it should be. Inherent in teaching is the call to see clearly, for without a clear perception of the past, present, and future, the teacher is unable to help the learner understand the continuity of the three. Without a clear vision, the teacher is unable to understand the world of the learner which influences the teaching/learning impulse.

Clear vision demands objectivity. Distorted perceptions, discouragements, and unrealistic thinking can hinder the educational process. We must equally see both the reality of the world and the reality of God. On one extreme, we may become too optimistic; on the other hand, we may become too pessimistic. A balance is needed in viewing reality. Only in our being objective can progress be made. Without objectivity, we may feel with the learner but not teach him or her.

Teaching is preparing the learner for a world that exists. Christian teachers who understand reality have an attractive quality, possessing a credibility that causes learners to return again and again for instruction. Seeing reality and being able to communicate that reality enhances learning. No one has had such a clear understanding and an ability to communicate reality as did Jesus Christ.

Scripture records that Jesus both perceived and taught reality. Jesus pointed out the inconsistencies and the consequences of behavior of the Pharisees and Sadducees. Clinging to religions traditions, the Pharisees had violated the spirit of God's message. Jesus said: "So, for the sake of your tradition, you make void the word of God. You hypocrites! Isaiah prophesied rightly about you when he said: 'This people honors me with their lips, but their hearts are far from me; in vain do they worship me, teaching human precepts as doctrines' " (Matt. 15:6-9).

To those who would learn and follow him, Jesus gave the opportunity to understand what would be required of them. He did not portray a relationship without cost. "He called the crowd with his disciples, and said to them, 'If any want to become my followers, let them deny themselves and take up their cross and follow me. For those who want to save their life will lose it, and those who lose their life for my sake, and for the sake of the gospel, will save it' " (Mark 8:34-35).

Jesus gave practical reality-based instructions to his followers as they left to minister to the lost world. These disciples were to seek receptive places in which to minister. If people or situations were non-receptive, the disciples were to move to other areas (Matt. 10:11-14). His predictions were accurate in what would happen to his disciples. He said, "See, I am sending you out like sheep into the midst of wolves; so be wise as serpents and innocent as doves. Beware of them for they will hand you over to councils and flog you in their synagogues; and you will be dragged before governors and kings because of me, as a testimony to them and the Gentiles" (Matt. 10:16-18). As teacher, Jesus saw the world and its needs and conveyed this reality to His learners. Jesus prepared His followers for the real world.

Acceptance of Persons and the World

Acceptance is one of the basic requirements for life to move forward. This principle applies not only to the spiritual, but also to every arena of life. For example, the adolescent must learn to accept his changing body if he is to develop a productive self-concept. If we are to move in relationship to God, we must accept Him and His commandments. In whatever activity we involve ourselves, there is the need for our own self-acceptance. A primary task of the teaching/learning process is helping learners accept themselves both in strength and in weakness.

Teachers have a pivotal place of responsibility and leadership. What we know about ourselves, about others, and about our world is influenced by the teachers we have experienced. Acceptance is contagious. If the teacher does not accept the learner as a person, it is impossible for the teacher to teach the learner self-acceptance. People learn to accept themselves by being accepted by significant others. Learners mirror what has been taught them by their teachers.

As an elementary school student, I was highly influenced by my sixth-grade teacher. I remember the ideas she spoke when describing communism. She clearly stated that the two Germanys would not be united. The Soviet Union would never permit the reunification because of the havoc reaped upon the Soviet Union by Germany in two world wars. However, in 1989, Germany was reunited. My first thoughts were: "This cannot happen; Mrs. Russell said it would never occur." As I listened to myself, I became increasingly aware of the powerful influence of my sixth-grade teacher. Her influence shaped much of my thinking and my self-acceptance. Teachers shape not only our acceptance of textbook knowledge, but also our self-acceptance.

Christian teachers, by profession of faith, are involved in sharing the gospel and in equipping others to share the gospel. Sharing the gospel involves accepting other people regardless of race, origins, or nationalities. Christians should not be selective in deciding with whom they will share the gospel. If we do practice selectivity in sharing the gospel, we may lose the opportunity and privilege of being partakers in the Great Commission. It is imperative that the Christian teacher have an acceptance of learners that is communicated to those learners. In turn, the learners may catch self-acceptance and develop an acceptance of others.

Before we accept someone else, we must first accept ourselves. Teachers cannot teach effectively without having accepted themselves. Acceptance of self involves having a proper respect and love for ourselves. Because God loves us enough to die for our sins, we need to love ourselves enough to live for Him. Out of this acceptance, we are challenged to love others. We can do many things because we are loved and because we love. This love was initiated and is sustained by Jesus Christ.

Acceptance was characteristic of the life of Jesus Christ. He accepted His mission and purpose in life; through the wilderness experience, He accepted the will of God. With each temptation, He came closer to God and the acceptance of His mission. Promises of bread, sensationalism, and compromise were met with a resolve to follow God's plan for His life. This testing strengthened and purified Jesus and demonstrated His submissiveness to the will of the Father.

Having accepted Himself and His mission, Jesus demonstrated His acceptance of self and others. For example, He could share joy at a wedding feast (John 2:1-11); lament for a lost city (Matt. 23:37); and mourn the loss of a friend (John 11:33). Jesus shared His authority with His disciples. "Then Jesus summoned his twelve disciples and gave them authority over unclean spirits, to cast them out, and to cure every disease and every sickness" (Matt. 10:1). To share authority and responsibility with others is one of the clearest demonstrations of genuinely accepting other people. Jesus accepted His disciples in both strength and weakness. By being accepted by the Master, these disciples could learn of Him and teach others of Him. Christian teachers must follow this same acceptance.

Lack of Pretense

Because we have accepted ourselves, we can provide those around us with a clear breath of fresh air or a sweet aroma. We do not have to mask our feelings, hide our motives, or change our identities. A great deal of energy is expended in pretending to be what we are not. We can avoid this wasted energy. Refreshingly, we can be who we are.

This freedom allows our behavior not to be strained or artificial. The behavior we choose involves our assuming responsibility for our actions. Being free and natural is no license to act irresponsibly. Rather, being free carries with it a high measure of responsibility and accountability. We are not locked into one rigid way of relating to others. We can conform our behavior when necessary. For example, in order to protect ourselves and others, we can "play by the rules."

Scripture records that Jesus went about doing good. Wherever He went, His life was natural, without pretense. Jesus had many facets or dimensions to His personality. In all that He did, He was still the same. Jesus taught great masses of people; he drove moneychangers from the temple; and He washed the feet of His disciples. In these encounters, Jesus acted naturally and without undue concern for what others thought. By acting naturally, He conveyed a sense of reality that was attractive to His followers. Jesus devoted energy to being who He was and not to who He was not. Such freedom and lack of pretense enhances the joy of teaching and the possibility of genuine learning.

Commitment to a Task

An important quality of any good teacher is the ability to center on a task. Centering on a task means devoting the needed time, energy, creativity and perseverance needed to complete the task. Commitment is seeing the job concluded; teaching involves such commitment. In a sense, the teaching task is never complete. With other endeavors, we may clearly see an end to the work. Although the individual teaching session may end, Christian teaching never ends.

Because it is a never-ending task, the teacher must realize the commitments needed in teaching others. Life-style is an important aspect of this commitment, both informally and formally, in and out of the classroom. In a real sense, the teacher never escapes the scrutiny of those around him.

Jesus devoted Himself to the mission of redemption that included teaching, preaching, and healing. His words on commitment were demanding and costly. To those who would delay commitment, Jesus was non-compromising. Jesus responded, "No one who puts a hand to the plow and looks back is fit for the kingdom of God" (Luke 9:62). Such a commitment involves that ability to discern the important from the trivial. Two sisters entertained Jesus in their home. Martha spent time preparing for a meal; Mary spent time listening to Jesus's teaching. When Martha complained about Mary not helping, Jesus said "Mary has chosen the better part, which will not be taken away from her" (Luke 10:42). Jesus instructed His followers to give priority to the important, not trivial matters.

Need for Rest, Reflection, and Revitalization

Teaching demands energy. After the first summer as a college freshman, I was enlisted as a youth teacher in Vacation Bible School. Although I thoroughly enjoyed the experience, I was exhausted. Looking back at the good teaching which I had experienced, I realized my teachers were probably exhausted at the end of the teaching period. Done properly, teaching is tiring because the teacher utilizes both energy and personality resources in the process. It is a "good" exhaustion, but exhaustion nevertheless.

In order to replenish themselves, teachers have a basic need for moments of privacy. This need allows for the needed personal reflection, evaluation of the teaching/learning process, and revitalization of energy. In my office, I have a placard that reads "Three Good Reasons For Teaching: June, July, and August." Not every teacher, especially those in church, can have three months of summer rest. However, each teacher needs periods of time away from teaching for renewal.

By nature of their task, teachers are givers to the community of faith. As individuals, teachers need periods in which they are the recipients. They need personal, as well as corporate worship. They need to be learners again. Being a part of a classroom situation provides teacher-enhancement as well as learner-enhancement. Teachers can view the teaching/learning process from the other side. In so doing, they may gain new insights, new techniques, and other ways to explore learning. We become better teachers when we ourselves are learners.

Like all individuals, teachers need daily periods of devotion for themselves. Time spent in quiet meditation and prayer provides the ability to deal with the concerns and chaos that arise in the teaching/learning situation. The teacher must take time for self; this is not selfish. The teacher who does not take periodic time for self limits his effectiveness as a teacher. While teachers in church may not spend hours each day teaching as does a public classroom teacher, they still have other demands on their time. Burnout will result without these periods of reflection, rest, and revitalization.

The need for rest, reflection, and revitalization was illustrated by Jesus. Jesus demonstrated His need to be alone by going to a quiet place to pray (Mark 1:35). In preparation for His greatest trial, He went to Gethsemane to pray and to renew Himself (Matt. 26:36). In like manner, Jesus instructed His disciples in their need to pray. Those who give need to be revitalized.

Independence of Culture and Environment

A good teacher is one who can teach beyond immediate circumstances. While the teacher must be aware of the importance of culture and environment, the teacher should be able to act independently of it when necessary. The ability to do this involves a belief in self, one's potentialities, and a well-developed theology. Unlike Esau, this person is not willing to sell his birthright for a bowl of soup. Going against culture may be important as displayed by Jesus.

Jesus was reared in the traditions of Jews that included circumcision (Luke 2:21); having been presented to the Lord (Luke 2:22); having been involved in observation of the Passover (Luke 2:41); and having studied in the temple (Luke 2:46-51). Luke 2:52 beautifully records Jesus' growth: "And Jesus increased in wisdom and in years, and in divine and human favor." Steeped in a religious community and tradition, Jesus was nevertheless able to be independent of that environment when necessary. For example, Jesus healed on the Sabbath, which was contrary to Jewish tradition (Mark 3:1-6). For Jesus, doing the will of God took precedence over the will, traditions, and culture of human beings. Teachers who demonstrate such qualities encourage learners to do likewise.

Attitude of Appreciation and Excitement

Good teachers are not bored with life; good teachers promote a new appreciation for living. This quality is one of attitude: something always to learn; something always to teach. Each part of life offers potential growth and challenge. Such an attitude promotes learner readiness and learner eagerness.

Emotions are a part of our human make-up. Teaching needs to provide enrichment for our emotions. This does not mean that teaching is exclusively emotional; however, when appropriate, the learning process allows for emotional growth and development. Praise, thanksgiving, wonder, hurt, and hope can be appropriately expressed in the learning environment.

Teachers should seek out experiences that will provide nourishment for their lives. This excitement may be found privately or publicly. These peak or mystic experiences should redirect the teacher back to the task in everyday living and teaching. Attending a conference, leading a seminar or reading an article can be an exciting encounter. Such peak experiences allow the teacher to deal with the other less exciting aspects of life.

In the midst of busy activity, Jesus was sensitive and aware of the small events that occur. However small, these incidents were life-changing. In a crowd of people, Jesus was aware of a woman who touched the hem of His garment. Turning toward her, He said her faith had made her well (Matt. 9:20-22). A short-statured tax collector, who thought he was unable to get the attention of Jesus, climbed a sycamore tree. Jesus not only stopped to notice Zacchaeus but also had fellowship in the home of this hated tax collector. Zacchaeus' life was changed. He said: "Look, half of my possessions, Lord, I will give to the poor; and if I have defrauded anyone of anything, I will pay back four times as much" (Luke 19:8). And Jesus responded, "Today salvation has come to this house, because he too is a son of Abraham" (Luke 19:9). Appreciation and excitement were natural attributes of Christ.

Interest in Social Issues

In Christian teaching, one objective is learner involvement in God's world. Learners become involved if teachers are involved. The teacher should be a spokesman for interest in the social issues of life which focus upon the needs of the learner and others around him. The teacher needs to be vitally interested in people and, in turn, with those social issues and concerns.

Having an interest in social concerns encourages the learner to explore the issues in the context of the learning. Such teaching is alive and challenging. Consequently, these learners may engage in personal ministry to such social concerns as poverty, illness, and discrimination. Modeled involvement by the teacher stimulates the involvement of others.

Jesus' life demonstrated one very much involved in the social concerns of people. Not only was there an involvement in spiritual concerns but also an involvement in concerns for physical welfare— feeding of people and healing of the sick; for the social prejudices— associating with the Samaritans and restoring the sick of the community. Jesus said "I came that they may have life, and have it abundantly" (John 10:10). The words "they" and "life" reflect a powerful magnitude of concern and opportunity for people.

Interest in Interpersonal Relations

Teachers, who by their vocation or avocation deal with people on an everyday basis, have an inherent need for close personal relationships. These friendships provide a source of satisfaction, insight, and direction for the individual's well-being. Generally, a concentrated investment of time and energy in friendships limits the number of close friends. However, these close friends provide significant strength.

Skills are needed in the forming of meaningful friendships. Friendships involve such qualities as honesty, feedback, availability, accepance, and dependability. Quality relationships must be reciprocal. Having a good support system can help encourage one in such service-oriented and energy-draining tasks as teaching. Build support groups among church teachers through teachers' meetings, fellowships, conferences, and every other opportunity where two or more teachers are gathered. When two or more teachers are gathered, let there be mutual support.

In large groups and in small groups, Jesus demonstrated His interpersonal relationship skills. Although He ministered to the large group, Jesus nevertheless had a more concentrated ministry with His twelve followers. In these twelve, He devoted time and energy. In an even smaller circle comprised of Peter, James, and John, Jesus developed more intense relationships. Such relationships shaped ministry and human destiny.

Willingness to Learn from All

The exceptional teacher has the desire to learn from all of his learners. Regardless of knowledge and ability, everyone has the potential to learn from everyone else. For such potentiality to be realized, one must listen, respect, and seek to understand the learner.

This teacher's willingness to learn enhances the learner's willingness to learn because the process becomes a cooperative effort. Both open-mindedness and people-mindedness are essential. Be open to learn from all regardless of background, circumstances, or structure. As a summer missionary to the Cayman Islands, I worked with a youth group in preparing a drama for the island. I was the playwright for the group. Everything was going wonderfully, I thought, until my cast members had a "few" suggestions. One scene I had so carefully written was not appealing to them. In fact, they said the play would work much better without the scene. At first, I was offended. How could these little "islanders" know more than I? As I thought more about it, I realized they were right and I was wrong. We did the play and it was successful, even without my carefully written scene. I learned the importance of learning from the learner.

Jesus's life demonstrated this willingness to learn. Jesus' parents discovered their Son in the temple. Like other Jewish children, Jesus received both religious teaching and vocational skills. In examining the adult life of Jesus, we can infer His willingness to learn from others. While Jesus had all knowledge at His disposal, He learned from the experiences of others. By identifying with people in their joy, their sickness, their goodness, and their sin, He learned more and more of the human condition. Learning from people and knowing them strengthened His ministry.

Discriminates Between Means and Ends

How easy it is to become so involved with the forest that one cannot see the trees. In teaching, it is essential that we know the difference between ultimate goals and the steps toward those goals. For example, is the ultimate goal to play Bible games or to impart Scriptural knowledge? If Scriptural knowledge is the goal, then the teacher may choose any number of means—lecture, discussion groups, case studies, or debates—to accomplish that end. If the teacher is unsure of the learning goal, what about the learner? Just as understanding encourages understanding, confusion encourages confusion.

Christian teaching/learning is directed toward individuals. The individual and his potential should be primary in the teacher's plan. The steps in the process must not become more important than the product. For example, do not rush to complete the "lesson," if there is a greater lesson to be taught that day. Take the time to listen and to observe the needs of the learners even as you teach. Their needs may take precedence over your well-planned lesson.

Remember you are there to teach people, not printed material. Flexibility provides that the various means, even well-planned ones, can be altered in order to accomplish the intended goal. Know the difference between the means and the ends.

No one knew better the distinction between the law and the spirit of the law than did Jesus. Once Jesus was accused of breaking the Sabbath by feeding His followers. This restriction and other laws had evolved with the intention of keeping the Sabbath. In the process, keeping the Sabbath had become a grueling task, and the original intent had been lost. Jesus helped to clarify the difference between means and ends by concisely stating, "The sabbath was made for humankind, not humankind for the sabbath; so the Son of Man is lord even of the sabbath" (Mark 2:27-28).

Sense of Humor

Laughter is said to be the best medicine. A good sense of humor is certainly an advantage for a teacher in building rapport between the teacher and learner. This type of humor involves being able to see the folly of the human state. We do not take ourselves so seriously that we cannot see our own eccentricities. Learn to laugh at yourself; learn to laugh at your mistakes.

Jesus must have had a sense of humor as He dealt with mankind. This humor was not a critical one, but one that acknowledged the folly of all people. Even in humor, Jesus was able to facilitate the teaching/learning process. In a parable, Jesus told about a man who foolishly built his house on the sand (Matt. 7:26). No doubt this elicited laughter on the part of the audience. However, this use of humor led to a greater spiritual truth. Various forms of conflict and adversity will come to all. Those whose lives have solid spiritual foundations will survive. Others will perish. Humor, as revealed in the parables, was a tool of teaching that gently illustrated spiritual truth.

Display of Creativeness

A good quality of a teacher is the ability to be creative. While creativity is important in terms of presentation, creativity means the freedom to be and to do many things. Being creative means being sensitive to life itself. Made in the image of God, all persons have varying degrees of creativity within them.

It is not surprising that creativity marked the life of Jesus. In all that He did, Jesus was creatively involved in the redemption of humanity. One example of this creativity is the ability to express the gospel in ways that communicated to various individuals. To the Samaritan woman at the well, Jesus spoke of "living water" (John 4:14); to Nicodemus, he spoke of "being born again" (John 3:3). Creatively, He communicated to those around Him. In describing the quality of faith to primarily an agrarian people, Jesus said "If you had faith the size of a mustard seed, you could say to this mulberry tree, 'Be uprooted and planted in the sea,' and it would obey you" (Luke 17:6-7). Jesus displayed creativity as He worked in and through the lives of people.

Looking Back

We may develop a wonderful repertoire of teaching methods and presentation techniques. These strategies, no matter how wonderful, can be quickly erased by our personality or our manner of presentation. As described in this chapter, one of the greatest assets for the teacher, as well as one of the greatest liabilities, is his or her personality.

Personalities are communicable. Students absorb the personality of the teacher. While certain personality traits may be inborn, personality is certainly modifiable. The following are suggested guidelines, derived from this chapter's analysis, for developing characteristics that may enhance effectiveness as a teacher and person.

1. Sharpen your perception of reality. Read and study both the Bible and the newspaper. Venture into life. Become actively involved in the world, a contributing part of God's creation. Every aspect of life has implication for the teacher as well as the learner. Encourage realistic thinking among students. Suggest books that will stimulate thinking. Provide experiences that will be life changing.

2. Accept both yourself and those around you. A teacher must accept himself before he can truly accept his learners. Your self-concept influences the way you behave toward other people. Do you need to forgive yourself? Do you need God's forgiveness? Do you need to forgive others? Remember that we are all created in the image of God. Do you have prejudices against certain people? How do stereotypes influence your acceptance of others? The more you get to know a person, the more likely you are to accept him as a person of value.

3. Be natural in who you are. Be genuine and natural in your conduct. Phoniness is easy to detect. Believing God accepts us gives us the freedom to be natural. No longer worry about who you are not; focus on the gift that is within you as a child of God. Only as we remove our pretenses can God work through us. People respond to those who are natural and sincere.

4. Commit to the task of teaching. Teaching is a tremendous task. If you make the commitment, follow through with appropriate actions. Do not focus on the trivial. Learn to say no. Be willing to make the sacrifices necessary for the task. Outline what it means to be committed to teaching. Discuss the requirements with others.

5. Plan for periodic times of rest and reflection. Daily time and special occasion time should be devoted to your own revitalization. Teaching calls for an expenditure of energy that must be replenished. Plan for your own renewal. Don't neglect your own worship experiences.

6. Act independently of convention when necessary. Rather than being a passive and conforming agent, the teachers should be an active and transforming agent in society. Confident of a higher loyalty, the teacher can go against the crowd when necessary. Learn to distinguish between what is person-ordained and what is God-ordained.

7. Develop an appreciation for every event in life. Every encounter, great or small, is significant. Excitement about living and learning will transfer to the learner. Share your excitement and appreciation with fellow church members.

8. Become personally involved in students' lives and social issues. The Christian gospel seeks to make a difference in the world of man. Isolated Christianity is not possible. To be a Christian is to become involved in social concerns and problems. Involve your learners in the various activities of the church both in and out of the church walls.

9. Develop close personal relationships with others. Relationships with significant others are nurturing, especially to those who by their jobs are nurturers. Those who are constantly giving also need to be recipients. These relationships can provide support, strength, and guidance. This type of quality relationship can minimize teacher burnout.

10. Be willing to learn from all. All people and situations are possible sources of new learning and insight. A willingness to learn from all reinforces the dignity of every person.

11. Know the difference between goals and the ways to obtain the goal. Is the goal to teach the Sunday School lesson (the quarterly) or to teach the student? Keep the goals clearly in mind. Review the goals periodically so that you do not become so involved in the small steps that you miss the ultimate end or goal.

12. Learn to laugh at yourself and situations. This laughter is not a critical one but one that laughs at the folly of man. Positive humor does not seek to degrade self or others. Positive humor keeps our spirits refreshed and our energies focused on the job at hand.

13. Develop a creative awareness for life. Let your natural curiosity keep you creative. Take chances. Seek to do what will best communicate in the teaching/learning process.

Looking Ahead

Congratulations, you have completed four steps in obtaining your passport to teaching. In this chapter, you have learned the importance of the qualities of the teacher to the business of learning. Only two more steps to complete. The next chapter will focus on lesson planning.

Notes

1. See Stella Chess and Alexander Thomas, *Temperament in Clinical Practice* (New York: Guilford, 1986) and "Temperamental Individuality From Childhood To Adolescence," *Journal of Child Psychiatry* 16 (1977), 218-226.

2. See Arnold Buss and Robert Plomin, *A Temperament Theory of Personality Development* (New York: Wiley-Interscience, 1984).

3. See Abraham H. Maslow, *Motivation and Personality* (New York: Harper & Row, 1970).

Learning Activities

1. "Teaching Personality"
A. Choose a teacher who has been the most influential in your life. Write down the qualities of that teacher. How did these characteristics contribute to the teaching/learning process? If possible, write a letter of appreciation to that teacher.
B. What qualities do you wish that you possessed. Write down specific ways that you might begin displaying these qualities. Pray for God's guidance and direction as you seek to develop these qualities in your life.

2. "Clear Sense of Reality"
A. Examine a recent newspaper or newsmagazine. List the current world events. Beside each event write how this event has significance for Christian teaching.
B. In a small group that you teach, give out a piece of drawing paper to each member. Provide the group with crayons, pencils, or drawing pens. Have each individual draw a picture of his world. Compare the pictures for similarities and differences.

3. "Acceptance of Persons and the World"
A. List four positive and four negative qualities about yourself. How do you feel about each of these qualities? Do these qualities influence how you accept yourself? What, if any, are the implications?
B. Think about your deepest prejudices, if any, that you have about people or situations. Do these prejudices influence how you live? If so, consider sincerely praying to God that these prejudices might be removed. Do not be surprised if God calls you to action.
C. "You cannot love others if you do not love yourself." Respond to the above statement. Why or why not? Be specific.

4. "Lack of Pretense"
A. Consult with a close friend. Ask if you display any pretentious (unreal, unnatural) behavior to people. If so, seek the advice of the friend as to how you might improve.
B. This week read one of the Gospels. Write down instances in which Jesus acted naturally and without pretense.

5. "Commitment to a Task"
A. Interview several teachers that you know. Ask each teacher the commitments necessary in being a teacher.

B. If you are a teacher in any church or secular educational function, list the responsibilities necessary to fulfill your teaching responsibility. Evaluate yourself on each responsibility in terms of (1) improvements needed; (2) doing a good job; and (3) doing an excellent job. Make a plan of action for improving.

C. If you are a teacher, create a weekly plan that prepares you for the week's lesson. List day-by-day what needs to be accomplished.

6. "Need for Rest, Reflection, and Revitalization"

A. What is the relationship between rest (quiet time) and the other activities of the day for you? Are there any implications?

B. Plan your week for both daily periods and other periods of renewal. Try this for one month. Does this make a difference in how you perform other duties?

7. "Independence of Culture and Environment"

A. Is there any conflict between being a good Christian teacher and being a supporter of cultural standards and expectations? Explain.

B. Examine your church and its various functions. What factors are man-ordained (instituted)? What factors are God-ordained (instituted)? Is it always easy to differentiate between the two? Why or Why not?

8. "Attitude of Appreciation and Excitement"

A. List the various activities of your day. How much of your day is routine? How much of your day is unusual? What is the difference between something being routine and something being unusual?

B. Create a greeting card to send to someone who has been important to you. Express appreciation for that person. Send the card.

C. Read the story of the good Samaritan (Luke 10:29-37). Describe the appreciation and excitement of each of those characters. What do you believe contributed to each acting in the manner recorded in Scripture?

9. "Interest in Social Issues"

A. Interview a teenager, a young adult, a middle aged adult and a older adult. Ask each what he believes to be the important social issues of today. How do their lists compare with your own ideas?

B. Examine the social issues prevalent in Jesus' day. Find evidence, if any, of how Jesus dealt with the concerns.

10. "Interest in Interpersonal Relations"

A. Describe your circle of close friends. What do these friends contribute to you? What do you contribute to these friends?

B. What do you believe were the contributions that Jesus' friends made to him?

C. In a small group or alone, devise guidelines that should give directions to interpersonal relationships.

11. "Willingness to Learn from All"

A. Imagine that you have been brought into a court room. The charge: you have been accused of being willing to learn from all. What types of evidence would be presented? Would you be found guilty? Why?

B. Each night for one week, spend time reflecting on how you learned from other people or situations. Be as specific as possible.

12. "Discriminates Between Means and Ends"

A. List people from the Bible who became confused with the difference between the ends and the means. What do you believe contributed to their confusion?

B. This week, examine the various activities that you engage in. Have you become confused between the goal and what you to do reach the goal? Have the means become more important than the end? What can you do to rectify the situation?

13. "Sense of Humor"

A. In what ways can humor contribute to the teaching/learning process? Can humor ever be a detriment to the teaching/learning process? How, if any, has humor contributed to your own learning? Explain.

B. Describe how teachers you have had used humor effectively in the classroom situation. What were the results? Describe how teachers have used humor inappropriately in the classroom situation. What were the results?

14. "Display of Creativeness"

A. Pretend that you are talking to an alien. Explain what creativeness is.

B. Discuss creativeness and the character of God.

5. Lesson Planning

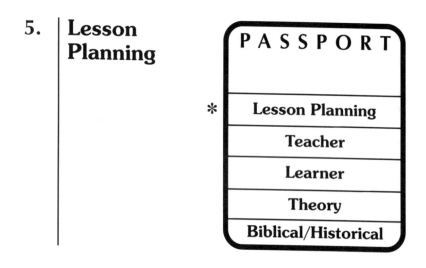

PASSPORT

* Lesson Planning

Teacher

Learner

Theory

Biblical/Historical

Establishing Importance

"Everyone wants to have a book published; however, no one wants to write a book." This idea is a striking truth in the field of writing. How many individuals do you know who have a book in their head? All they need to do is put it down on paper. Well, putting the book on paper is the hardest yet most essential element in getting a book published. Many would be published; few would be writers.

The same comparison may be said for teaching. Many individuals may aspire to be teachers; however, few are willing to plan their lessons and teaching strategies. Planning a lesson on paper brings the possibility of an effective lesson one step closer to reality. Planning a lesson gives the teacher confidence and freedom to focus attention upon the learner in the teaching/learning process.

Defining Chapter Goals

Now you will study the fifth element, lesson planning, in order to obtain your passport to teaching. Your study will involve the pre-steps to lesson planning; the construction of the lesson plan; and implementing the lesson plan. At the conclusion of this chapter, you should be able to do the following:

- identify and describe five pre-steps to the lesson planning process;
- list various resource tools to preparing a lesson;
- describe the importance of a lesson goal and two sources for formulating the goal;
- list steps in reaching a lesson goal;
- identify three common parts of a learning activity; and
- list six guidelines for implementing a lesson plan.

Pre-Steps to Lesson Planning

While you may simply sit down and begin writing a book, other approaches involve doing preliminary work. For example, the writer may want to find the intended audience, the literary category, the characters, the conflicts, or the length. This preliminary work illustrates an organized and, perhaps, a more effective literary process. If a destination is known, plans can be made to reach it. While the writer may stop and do more reflection and research in the writing process, he has the basic materials and orientation to begin writing. As in writing, pre-steps in lesson planning provide the necessary building foundations for the teaching/learning process.

Analyze the Material

In any teaching/learning process, the teacher must initially examine the material to be presented. The material may be a text from the Bible, a section from a book, a practical experience from life, or a case study. Whatever the content, the teacher must become as thoroughly familiar with the material as possible. To the best of your ability, you become the expert. Regardless of how little you initially know, with preparation you will know more than the majority of your learners.

Various tools can make the research process much easier for analyzing the material. In Bible study, for example, sources to consult include various commentaries (the lesson quarterly is a commentary); a Bible dictionary; a Bible map or atlas; a concordance; and a study Bible. Each of these study aids provide specialized helps to the teacher/learner. The more sources you are able to consult, the greater the possibility for gaining a deeper measure of understanding.

In this step, as in all other steps, seek the wisdom of the Holy Spirit. Ask the Lord to direct you to understand the material and the message that He would have you teach. By submitting yourself to Him, you bring yourself closer to understanding His revealed truth not only for yourself but also for your learners.

As the teacher studies, he may become personally challenged in some way with the material. Share your own growth of study with the class members. Personalize the lesson first in your life; this step will lend itself to greater personalization in the lives of others. Learning to model what is taught is one of the most powerful testimonies to having studied the material.

Analyze the Learner

As I type these words on my word processor, you-the-reader sit on top of my word processor. At least, you sit there in my imagination. In order to communicate more effectively with you, I try to understand your needs, struggles, and questions. In the same way, approach the lesson planning process. Mentally have your learners sit next to you. Keep them in mind in planning the process.

Examine the needs of the class members or the learner audience. Look at their struggles developmentally. What is the relevancy of this material for the intended learners? What do they need to gain from this material? Examine their cognitive level (intellectual or educational), social level, emotional level, physical level, and spiritual level. Are they ready to be challenged intellectually? What are their specific social needs? Are they mature or immature Christians? These types of questions facilitate the construction of a good lesson.

In any learning situation, there are a great variety of individuals. Consequently, some learners may be challenged; others may be bored. Try to plan a lesson that will have some relevancy for each one. While each individual may be at a different point in his spiritual life, each one has a spiritual need. Try to make the gospel real in ways that are supportive to all class members.

Analyze Previous Study or Experiences

A good writer does not write parts of a story in isolation; rather, there is a progression and development from one section of the story to another. A good teacher knows that one teaching/learning situation does not exist in isolation. Rather, teaching/learning is built upon previous weeks of study and various experiences of the learner.

Capitalize upon this idea in your lesson planning. Relate how this week's lesson is related to past studies. Show the future development.

Demonstrate how this lesson will be expanded next week. If someone has experienced a personal crisis (death, loss of job, birth of a child), relate this experience to the lesson if appropriate. Be sensitive, making sure your comments are suitable for all concerned. This process allows the learner to discover that lessons build upon previous lessons. It shows that the learning process is heading somewhere, rather than just filling isolated blocks of time. Learning is both lifelong and life related.

If possible, relate previous comments or testimonies of the members to the current lesson under study. Again this shows the relevancy of the past to the present teaching moments. Furthermore, it demonstrates that you listen and remember the comments or questions of class members. Learners become more attentive when they know the teacher cares and listens.

Analyze Special Circumstances or Conditions

Be aware of the current events both in your church and in your community, as well as the greater world. These special conditions may prove valuable as you seek to make the lesson have application and relevancy for the learner. Several weeks before Christmas, I gave a devotional in a Sunday School department during foreign mission emphasis. Having served as a missionary for two years, I was aware of the importance of mission giving, as well as the material blessings of many Christians in the United States. I made the statement: "Remember, this year as you have brightly wrapped packages under the Christmas tree and wonderful meals at Christmas, there will be some people who will not have water for Christmas."

Mentally, I was recalling the hungry, desperate faces of those who lived in the drought-stricken parts of Africa. I then challenged the hearers to give generously to the mission offering. Within a month, what I spoke became a reality for those in the room. Several weeks later, we experienced a tremendous freeze in the area. Many in that Sunday School department did not have water for several days at Christmas. Later, I was able to use the story to illustrate that as we pray and give, we do not know the full impact of those prayers. We cannot presume upon God's goodness or the continuation of present-day luxury. Life can change in a matter of moments. Daily keeping our perspectives on God will prepare us for the unexpected.

Use contemporary situations, such as social problems or world events, to help illustrate the relevancy of God's Word. Help learners to experience God's working today by sharing appropriate life experiences. The God of the Old Testament and New Testament is still the God of our day. The teacher can vividly illustrate this relevancy by sharing his own understanding of how God works.

Analyze Organizational Structure

The organizational structure under which any teaching/learning occurs impacts the planning process. This structure may be a Sunday School, a one-hour discussion group, or a discipleship training retreat. While we desire freedom in learning, we are not fully free. We operate under a set of restrictions in teaching, just as we do in everyday life: being at work at a given time or paying bills on a given day. In all teaching/learning sessions, there are inherent restrictions that must be acknowledged.

Time.—Be respectful of the time allotted for the teaching. If you are given forty minutes, use the forty minutes effectively. Do not habitually go beyond the time allotted. Honor the time that you have been given by being prepared and by respecting the time of the learner.

The time allotted has an influence on what can reasonably be accomplished in a teaching/learning situation. As you plan, keep the time in mind. Plan for meaningful activities to encompass the allotted time. Estimate the time for the various components of the session. Should the lesson be concluded early, do not go back and "re-serve" the lesson in an attempt to fill up the time. Learners are aware when teachers do this maneuver. Simply dismiss the class and let the members fellowship if they like. Conclude the lesson when it is concluded. Experience will help any teacher in becoming a more effective time manager.

Purpose.—Keep in mind the purpose of the organization and its teaching opportunity. Organizational purposes can be used to guide the teaching/learning sessions. If the organization's purpose is to impart knowledge, let the experience do so in an effective and productive manner. If the purpose is to include fellowship and support, help these aspects become a natural and integral part of the learning experience. If the purpose is community or mission service, try to have some type of mission involvement, either direct or indirect, each time the group meets. Keeping the organizational purpose in mind can guide steps in teaching.

Restraints.—Be aware of any physical or other restraints in the teaching situation. This analysis can include anything from the seating arrangement to the availability of materials. Do not plan to use an overhead projector if the room lacks electrical outlets. If you are unsure of your surroundings, keep both materials and presentation simple. Try to avoid letting the structure "catch you off guard." Visit the teaching area prior to the session. Plan for the unexpected. Alternate or contingency plans of teaching can be both "face-saving" and "learner saving."

Lesson Planning

Once the pre-lesson planning has been completed, turn to planning the actual teaching/learning experience.

Define the Goal or Intent

One of the chief strengths of the lesson plan is the specific identification of goals for the teaching/learning session. Regardless of the type of teaching/learning, clearly defined goals enrich the experience for both learner and teacher. The goal shapes and directs the flow of the lesson. Without a goal, there is no specific direction for both teacher and learner.

Lesson goals emerge from two basic sources—needs of the learner and the material under investigation. The lesson goal should be what the learner will achieve; this may refer to knowledge, understanding, attitude, or skill. In studying the biblical material, goals may emerge from the intersection of the life needs of the learner and the truths of Scripture. As these areas are examined, the lesson goal emerges. *Effective goals are developed by thoroughly knowing both the learner and the material.* In order to define the learning goal, the following questions may be appropriate: What should the learners gain from this teaching/learning session? What should the learners feel from this teaching/learning session? What should the learners be able to do after this teaching/learning session? These types of questions may help clarify the construction of learning goals.

For example, if the lesson passage is on Jesus' feeding the five thousand (John 6:1-14), several possible lesson goals could emerge. You might have the learners list what Jesus did: He used what He had, gave thanks to God, and shared what He had. This goal becomes clear from the studying of the lesson. If you want your lesson goal to be more personal, you might have the learners identify what they own personally that they could give to God, such as time, talents, or opportunities.

Another lesson goal may be to have the adults in your class perform one activity this week in which they can share what they have with others. These types of goals make the lesson meaningful and directional.

As the teacher identifies the goal, specific ways should be developed that show how the goals will be reached. Some type of evaluation is essential. Complete evaluation will not always be possible in one teaching session. What should happen in the lives of individual learners to give evidence of successful teaching/learning? How will you know when the goal has been achieved? How you answer the foregoing questions forms the basis of evaluation.

Certain goals are easier to evaluate than others. For example, knowledge is relatively easy to achieve, measure, and evaluate. Goals involving attitude and behavioral life-style are much more difficult to evaluate. These goals may not easily be measured in one or even several learning sessions. Nevertheless, these are worthwhile ones to pursue, especially in Christian teaching/learning.

Develop Steps in Reaching the Goal

Now that the goal is firmly established, decide and develop steps that will lead to the successful completion of the goal.

Secure interest.—The opening of the lesson, as well as points throughout the lesson, must secure the interest or attention of the learner. Without the attention of the learner, all else is limited in possibility. Suggested ways to stimulate interest include the use of the paradox; the use of objects to provoke interest; the use of questions; the use of drama to depict the theme of the lesson; and the use of life needs or situations of the learner.

Construct appropriate learning activities.—Once the interest or focus of attention has been secured, the individual should then be directed toward appropriate learning activities. The next chapter will describe in greater detail the importance of appropriate learning activities. However, learning activities should be chosen in light of the developmental level of the learner, the type of material being studied, and the desired teaching/ learning goal.

These learning activities should lead gradually and naturally to the achieving of the stated teaching/learning goal. Regardless of the type of activities chosen, each should have these common elements: input, response, and feedback. Input involves the presentation of information and material to the learner. Input may be in the form of a lecture, discussion questions, directions, materials for an art activity, or a dramatic monologue. Input is the presentation of some "information."

Following input, response is necessary. This response involves the active involvement of the learner. Effective learning necessitates some type of learner involvement. After response, feedback is essential. Feedback involves the learner's giving evidence to what has been achieved. Feedback also involves the teacher's making response to the learner. Such response can confirm, guide, or redirect the learner and learning. Without feedback, both the learner and the teacher are at a loss in terms of what has actually transpired in the learning process.

Use transitions.—In writing, transitions make the connection between ideas or between paragraphs. In addition, transitions make possible the connecting among the various learning activities. Transitions help both the teacher and the learner by summarizing and guiding to the next activity. Transitions make the flow of the lesson and the teaching of the material easier.

Allow closure.—Each teaching/learning session demands some type of closure. Closure involves "putting it all together." Too often lessons are left hanging in mid air with no definite ending. Closure can serve various functions: summarize the lesson; review the key elements; apply the lesson content to daily life; provide assignments until the next teaching session; and anticipate what future teaching/learning sessions will explore. If teaching/learning is like a wrapped gift, closure is the ribbon that ties the package together.

Materials Needed

In lesson planning, the teacher should secure in advance any special materials that will be needed for the lesson. These materials may include posters, overhead transparencies, case studies, surveys, art supplies or other handouts. Once a colleague found me creating a poster for a class lecture. He asked, "Do you really think those things help?" Surprised by his question, I simply responded, "Yes, I do."

Indeed, materials prepared for a lesson are highly significant such as charts, posters, pictures, diagrams, typed directions, listening guides, and art materials. First, they allow the teacher freedom in the lesson. The teacher is less preoccupied with details if he has materials already prepared. Second, planned materials aid in the actual presentation of the lesson. Third, they demonstrate to the learner that you have spent time in preparation; this lesson has importance. The learner is important.

Fourth, prepared materials enhance the quality of the learning and the possibility of retention. Materials that capture the learner's interest and his involvement facilitate learning. The greater the active involvement of the learner, the greater likelihood of recalling information and the transfer of learning.

As the teacher prepares or considers preparing materials, the following questions may help. Will these materials make the learning more interesting? Will these materials make the learner more involved in the study? Will these materials encourage greater retention and application? Materials are not busy work; they are purposeful. Try to bring together all the materials that are necessary for the learner. Create and prepare materials for the learner and his learning. This preparation actively demonstrates the high priority of both the learner and the teaching/learning process.

Lessons Implementation

Now that the lesson plan has been prepared, the next step is implementation, practicing what has been prepared. The following guidelines will help in implementing or demonstrating the lesson.

- Secure attention at the beginning of the lesson. This first impression will create an attitude of excitement and draw subsequent attention to the materials at hand. Be on time and prepared to begin. Energizing your initial teaching moments will energize and direct the learner. Act alive and alert. Use your personality to attract and interest the learner.

- Personalize the learning activities. While the learning activities have been previously selected, each should be adapted to the actual learners present. Where possible, call upon individuals by name in the learning activities. Make references to positive information about the learners. Conduct these activities in an exciting and worthwhile manner. Explain the relationship of these learning activities to the lesson.

- Use Transitions. Use transitions to gently move from one activity to the next. Transitions may range from single words to phrases or to sentences. These "words" keep the momentum of the lesson strong.

- Apply the lesson, through transitions and learning activities, to the everyday experiences of the learner. Wherever and whenever possible, make the lesson relevant. Apply the lesson throughout the session, not just at the end.

- Focus upon the learner. Thorough preparation and familiarity with the lesson give the teacher freedom to focus upon the learner. Ideally, teachers teach learners, not material. Don't allow the quality of your materials to detract from the importance of the learner. He or she is more important than anything else you might do. Put the materials away if they detract from your concentrating on the learner. The teacher who knows the material can devote greater attention communicating to the unique qualities of the learners present.
- Be flexible. Adapt the lesson to newly discovered learner needs and other changing circumstances. Even in the middle of a lesson, significant insights and new needs may emerge. The teacher needs to be flexibly sensitive to focus on the greater lessons of the day. Again flexibility allows you to concentrate on the learner. The greatest lesson is the learner.

Looking Back

Lesson plans are prepared to facilitate the teaching/learning process. Although they provide structure, these plans are not intended to be followed without flexibility. Lessons plans are not written in concrete. Rather, these plans may be modified in light of new needs and situations. Changes should not be made in a haphazard or careless manner. Kept alive and open, these plans provide guidelines which will best facilitate teaching and learning.

Looking Ahead

Well done. You have completed the fifth element to obtain your teaching passport. Now you will study the sixth element, motivation and teaching/learning. Once you have completed chapter 6, you will be ready to visit various destinations of teaching/learning. Keep up the good work.

Notes

1. See Leroy Ford, *Design for Teaching and Training: A Self Study Guide to Lesson Planning* (Nashville: Broadman, 1978).

Learning Activities

1. "Case Study"
   The week-end teacher raining retreat was approximately three quarters complete. The class had spent the entire weekend

studying the elements of the teaching/learning process. Ample time was spent in the construction of learning goals. Opportunities were given for questions. Demonstrations abounded.

Tim, a quiet participant who taught junior high boys, approached the conference leader. "I know we have been studying the lesson planning process for the past two days." He paused.

"Is there a problem, Tim?" the teacher asked.

"Well, I just can't seem to get this lesson planning process. It is so different from the way I normally teach a class. I just don't see the reasons for the planning."

Not trying to take the remarks too personally, the teacher responded, "Explain to me, how you normally would teach a lesson, Tim."

Tim began, "Well, I study the lesson. And then I just talk the lesson through with the kids. Their questions lead me along as I talk. These lessons are successful. Last time I taught this way, two youth were converted."

A. If you were the teacher, what would your response be to Tim?

B. What assumptions may Tim be making about the lesson planning process?

C. What would you say or do in order to convince Tim of the importance of lesson planning?

D. Is Tim's attitude typical of Christian teachers? Why or Why not?

E. Is Tim's attitude typical of your church's attitude toward lesson planning? If so, what could you suggest as a way of changing that attitude?

2. "Pre-Steps in Lesson Planning"

A. Are there actual pre-steps in lesson planning? Are the pre-steps an actual part of the lesson planning process? Explain.

B. Explain in your words what is essential in this pre-step process of lesson preparation.

C. What would you add that was omitted from this section? Explain.

D. What is the value of this phase of preparation? Be as specific as possible.

E. Choose any lesson topic or theme that you wish. Go through the various steps in this phase with a specific group of learners in mind. Keep this information gathered for later use.

3. "Lesson Planning"

A. Based upon the information provided in the text, construct a sample lesson plan that could be followed. (In this activity, you are simply providing the categories for the lesson plan.)

B. In your own words, describe the importance of a teaching/learning goal.

C. What is the role of the transitions in the lesson planning process?

D. What is the importance of closure in a lesson?

E. Create a poster to depict the parts of a learning activity. Illustrate each part with a specific example.

4. "Lesson Implementation"

A. Select a Sunday School lesson and prepare a lesson plan according to the plan given.

B. Select a teacher whom you trust to view you as you teach the lesson to a group. Ask for feedback from the teacher in ways to improve your effectiveness.

C. Create an original lesson plan model based upon what you consider the essentials of a good lesson. Share your model with another individual and request constructive criticism.

6. Motivation and Teaching/ Learning

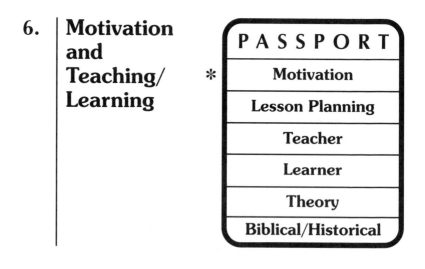

*

PASSPORT
Motivation
Lesson Planning
Teacher
Learner
Theory
Biblical/Historical

Establishing Importance

The bell had sounded signifying the end of the Sunday School hour. Into the hall went both teachers and learners. Most people went on to the church auditorium, and a few went for their cars. Two teachers headed for the parking lot.

"How can I get those students to learn? They don't want to try," Mrs. Carpenter said as she tossed her Bible in the backseat of her car.

"I know what you mean, I use the same methods that have worked so well for years. Now, the kids don't respond. I blame it on the parents," responded Mrs. Huff. Their heads nodded in unison as both ladies got into Mrs. Carpenter's car.

"I wonder what the special is at the cafeteria?" Mrs. Huff said.

"We'll find out soon. I sure do enjoy beating the rush, don't you," Mrs. Carpenter said as she drove off the parking lot.

Meanwhile, inside the auditorium, the minister of education began to welcome those who were in the congregation and to give a brief Sunday School report.

The above scenario illustrates a key aspect of learning—motivation. Motivation operates within a person and causes him or her to act in specific ways. Actors often ask writers and directors what motivates the characters they create. Theoretically, if motivation is understood, the actors can portray more accurately their characters. Either in real life or in a drama, behind our words and actions lie our motives. Whatever we do and wherever we go, motivation is a part of our lives. Both teachers and learners deal with the issues of motivation. Why should I learn? Why should I teach? Why won't people respond to what I teach? Why can't I do better? Should I take it personally if my students are not motivated to learn? Is motivation a quality that you have or don't have? Is motivation something that can willfully be chosen? Can motivation be communicated? These motivation-oriented questions surround the teaching/learning process.

Motivation is like a kaleidoscope. One turn in the kaleidoscope produces a new design or picture. Similarly, one change in motivation, whether it be in the teacher, the learner, or the teaching/learning method, produces a change in the whole pattern of teaching/learning. Each part of the learning system must deal with its own contribution to motivation. No one individual or part of the system contributes exclusively to motivation.

Defining Chapter Goals

In this chapter, you will obtain the sixth element—motivation—necessary for obtaining your teaching/learning passport. We will explore such issues as how a teacher becomes motivated; how teachers can motivate learners; establishing a motivational climate; choosing teaching methods; and using teaching methods to reach learning goals. At the conclusion of this chapter, the learner should be able to do the following:
- describe how a teacher can motivate him/herself;
- identify nine ways to motivate learners;
- describe how to create a motivational climate for learning;
- list four questions to ask when selecting an appropriate teaching method;
- identify ways to teach for knowledge;
- identify ways to teach for understanding;
- identify ways to teach for attitudes and values; and
- identify ways to teach for motor skills.

How a Teacher Motivates the Instructor

An effective teacher must be a highly motivated individual. It may be impossible to motivate someone to learn an idea or to gain a skill if the teacher is not committed. The teacher stimulates and motivates students indirectly through the developing of the teacher's own motivations. The following guidelines may help increase teacher motivation.

Respect Your Needs

Teachers have physical, social, emotional, psychological, and spiritual needs. The teacher must devote time to meeting his individual needs. If these needs are not met, the teacher is not going to be prepared to motivate others.

Respecting and meeting your needs is not selfish. Instead, it demonstrates respect for yourself and respect for the role you share in the lives of your learners. Having spent time alone in prayer, meditation, and study, Jesus was able both to motivate and to guide others. Meeting your own needs enables you to meet the needs of others more effectively.

If you fail to meet your own needs in a healthy fashion, your behavior will either consciously or unconsciously be directed toward meeting those needs. Take the example of sleep. Failing to get adequate sleep and rest diminishes both energy and enthusiasm for teaching. Rather than focusing on the teaching/learning process, our bodies begin slowing down, proving our urgent need for rest. If we fail to receive emotional or social support outside the classroom, we may consciously turn to our students as the primary sources of comfort and consolation. This process, called counter-transference in counseling, is not healthy. We "use" our students for our own basic needs; we do not focus upon our primary role as teacher.

These two examples illustrate the need for having our own needs met. Failing to have needs met outside class, the teacher turns the classroom, intentionally or unintentionally, into sources for meeting their unmet needs. Having needs met allows for focusing on the teaching/learning task. A balance can then be achieved in meeting your needs and the needs of others.

Prepare Adequately

As a rule, I love the teaching opportunity. However, I hate teaching when I am not prepared for the assignment. Being prepared for the teaching/learning process will greatly enhance your motivation in the process. When we are unprepared, the task is unpleasant. If we are on the edge of our seats waiting for the bell or buzzer to announce the end of Sunday School, we are not motivating our learners. Being adequately prepared will motivate you to do your best in the current moment because you already have the background information. Preparation does not come about without time and work. Being a quality teacher is a demanding process; it takes work. Learning to set priorities in preparation is essential. Learning to say "yes" and learning to say "no" will make all the difference in your motivation. You may not be able to spend Saturday night socializing if that takes away from your being awake for teaching the morning lesson. You may have to discipline yourself to study the lesson each day rather than cramming it all in on Saturday night at midnight. Good teachers learn to say "no" in order to say "yes" to their preparation and their personal needs.

Motivate Through Fellowship

The fellowship that you keep can either increase or decrease your motivation. A brilliant and compassionate teacher whom I know instructs her public school student-teachers that you do not find the best teachers in the teachers' lounge. The teachers' lounge may discourage motivation. While we do not have a teachers' lounge in church, we can gain insight into what my friend is saying.

Choose to be around people who are motivated and are motivating. Learn from these people how to act in motivational ways. We tend to become like the people with whom we associate. If you are around discouraging people, you tend to be discouraged. If you are around happy people, you tend to be happy. Carefully select the people with whom you associate. Their level of motivation will quickly become your level of motivation, either positively or negatively.

Remember "Your Call"

Being called of God to be involved in the teaching/learning process is significant. Without remembering and practicing our call, we may forget the reason for all that we do. Throughout the biblical message, the people are called to remember what God has done for them and what God has called them to be. Remembering your call will motivate you to do your best. Out of this sense of gratitude and responsibility, we will naturally motivate ourselves and others. Having been loved, accepted and called enables the teacher to love, accept, and to call out others.

Choose to Motivate

We can choose to motivate ourselves. If we wait until we feel like getting up and preparing the lesson, chances are we will stay in bed and the lesson will not be prepared. Rather than waiting for a mystic force to motivate us, we can choose to act. One counseling adage is, "It is easier to act your way into a new kind of feeling than to feel your way into a new action." Study the lesson, even when you do not feel like it. Invite someone to your class, even when you're busy with other activities.

Waiting to become motivated will not work. Rather, get up! Begin the process. As you begin to take the minor steps in doing a task, you will self-generate and build upon your motivation. The first steps are usually the most difficult. Later steps are dependent upon the first steps taken. Now start motivating yourself!

How a Teacher Motivates Learners

As you motivate yourself, you are in a much better position to motivate your learners. Being motivated compels us to share our interest enthusiastically with others. The following guidelines may serve as beginning points in directing motivation in your learners.

Focus on Learner Needs

As you seek to motivate others, you must focus upon their particular developmental and personal needs. This emphasis requires knowing not only developmental psychology but personally knowing your students. Although much information can be gathered from textbooks, some information must be taken from one-on-one contacts. Each person is different with unique needs.

If your learners have a deficiency in any area, you should seek to satisfy that deficiency. It is difficult to teach a Bible story to someone with an empty stomach. Provide a morning "mini-breakfast" in Sunday School or Vacation Bible School if needed. If there is pain over the breaking up of a marriage, it is difficult to expect effective committee work. Arrange for family counseling opportunities; be willing to listen. Enhance the motivation of others by being aware of their basic needs and concerns. Take time to know, to feel, and to act in light of their needs.

Meeting these needs may not always be done in the church setting of teaching/learning. Meeting unmet needs may involve work outside the church. Meeting needs is ministry; Christian teaching involves Christian ministry. Telephone conversations, cards, visits, and forms of other assistance may be necessary. Class members should be involved in ministry to the needs of those in and out of their class.

If these needs are being met, there will be greater likelihood of motivation and commitment to the teaching/learning process. Teaching becomes a joint ministry. Ministry may lead to life-changing decisions, a goal of Christian teaching.

Inspire Through Relationships

One primary way of motivating others is through the basic relationships found in the teaching/learning process. You may have had the experience of being with someone for whom you would do anything. If the person were to say, "Jump," our immediate response is, "How high?" Relationships motivate.

People are more motivated if significant relationships are being established and nurtured in the teaching/learning process. Feeling a part of the group encourages working toward the task of the group. If everyone is considered important with valuable contributions, greater learning and accomplishments may occur.

If everyone is made to feel that it is his or her class, the group is on its way to meeting its goals. Time spent in sharing hurts, dreams, and problems builds motivational strength in the group. If we have devoted time and energy, we are more likely to grow. Once in my first year of teaching, I was critical of a group to which I belonged. My attitudes, thoughts, and words were negative. Fortunately, I made a conscious effort to change. As I reinvested my energies into the group, my attitude gradually changed. The more I invested, the better my motivation developed. My negative criticisms diminished because this group was a part of me.

Involve Through Participation

We are motivated to work harder if we believe that we have some degree of participation in the setting of goals. If the goal or task becomes our own, we will devote more energy to its successful completion. As in the above example, the more I participated, the more I wanted to give to the group. In turn, the group gave back to me.

Feeling joint ownership of the teaching/learning process encourages all to be responsible for what happens. Involve people. If the teaching is poor, what can I do to help? If there are unmet needs, what can I do to help? By our involvement, we assume an active rather than a passive learning role. Active learning involves commitment and subsequently greater behavioral change.

Concentrate on Learner Interests

By focusing upon the interests of the individual, we are more prone to secure his attention. Interest must incorporate two aspects: the presentation itself must be interesting, and the interests of the learners must be used not only in the teaching methodology but also in the learning content. If John is interested in history, point out the historical backgrounds of the Bible passage. Mary's interest in homemaking may be a way of involving her in a ministry to the disadvantaged. Mrs. Jones may be noted for her ability to organize, which the mission committee could use in its survey work. Use interest to involve people in learning and serving.

Persuade Through Challenge

Individuals have an innate desire to be challenged in some particular direction. Some learners are challenged to build wells for the needy in a foreign country; others are challenged to give financially to world missions. Presenting a need, such as a chairperson for the evangelism committee or worker in the preschool area, challenges and motivates some individuals. Effective challenges are personal.

If we offer learners a challenge, they may be more likely to commit energy to meeting the challenge. Place realistic goals before the learner; stimulate her to work and to do well. In fact, challenges should vary just as the nature of the learner varies. Challenges should challenge but not overwhelm. With each challenge, a way of realistic success must be provided. Extra feedback and guidance may be necessary.

To challenge means to be available in time and resources to help meet the challenge. If you challenge your learners to explore why righteous people suffer, be there to assist. Provide Scripture readings and other inspirational books. Let them talk to those who have suffered and remained faithful to God. Listen to their questions and answers they may discover. Don't put them out on a limb and leave them. Be actively present as they venture into new areas of growth and maturity. Knowing that someone is there to guide and encourage makes the journey easier.

Engage in Self-Disclosure

By sharing personal struggles, both victories and defeats, you will motivate others to do likewise. If you can explain how you personally have grown through an experience, such as an illness or a financial difficulty, you may provide the needed incentive for others. Learn to share what is appropriate for the immediate teaching/learning task.

With the self-disclosure of other learners and teachers, the mood is set for the learner's potential self-disclosure. Share your life before and after becoming a Christian. What has been easy? What has been hard? Ask the learner if he or she has had such an experience. Appropriate and gradual self-disclosure motivates others to participate and to grow.

Concentrate on Application

Teachers can motivate others by showing the importance and application of what is being taught and learned. If we can show not only by words but also by deeds the answer to the question "So What?" we will make tremendous advances in the learning process. If a scriptural truth is shared, involve the learners in applying its truth to everyday life. If the Scripture deals with resolving conflicts, provide case studies appropriate for the learners. Ask how its truth can help Julie in dealing with work in computers, how it applies to Megan's work as a pharmacist, or how it has value to Tom as a single parent. These techniques will help "put the truth" into a real-life situation. What is taught becomes meaningfully related to everyday life experiences. Application convinces people.

Motivate Through Reinforcement

Reinforcement is a way of either increasing or decreasing behavior by providing special attention to the behavior. While positive reinforcers (something added to a behavior, such as a word of praise) increase desired behavior, negative reinforcers (something taken away, such as a privilege) decrease the undesirable behavior.

If a child in a Bible memorization class gives a correct response or acts in a positive way, the teacher may reinforce by praise, a "star" near his name on the poster, or a smile. By such rewards, the teacher is hoping the learner will continue to memorize Bible verses. If the learner's response or behavior is inappropriate, such as hitting another child, the teacher may take away a privilege in the hopes of altering that behavior. When used properly, reinforcements can be used to shape and modify behavior.

Encourage Through Explanation

If we know the reason why, we can endure almost any what. As the learner matures, he becomes increasingly sensitive to the why behind the what that is being taught. Sunday School teachers may be accused of giving assignments that are busy work, especially to youth. We may remember teachers who had us fill in the crossword puzzle, make a poster, or underline ideas on a sheet. It seemed like just plain busy work. Had the teacher given a little more explanation about what we were doing, it could have made a difference. Crossword puzzles are a good way to learn names of Bible heroes; posters can be used in another department to share what we are learning; and underlining key ideas helps us to be understand the Bible.

Attitudes and potential learning can change if the teacher explains the reason behind the work. Just as parents must explain behavioral requirements to adolescents, the teacher must explain to youth and adults about learning. Share the purpose behind the activity or the way the activity will benefit the learner. Explanations can be potent in motivating learning. Make sure there is a good reason for the work being done.

Motivational Climate

Motivational climate refers to conditions that encourage teaching and, in turn, learning. Robert Hawley identified three factors in establishing a positive motivational climate: goals for the class; procedures for reaching the goals; and general conditions within the classroom.[1] Perception is crucial. Both learners and teachers must have a mutually accurate perception of these three aspects. Each must know the goals, the procedures, and the rules. When teachers and learners honestly participate together in establishing these components, high motivation is more likely to occur.

Ideally, goals are established by both teacher and learner. Share with the learner what you hope to accomplish in the class. Ask the learners what they wish to gain from Bible study, what skills they need to develop, and what questions they may need answered. For example, the class may wish to learn more about the meaning of certain Bible passages; the teacher may wish that the class would engage in more outreach and ministry. Working together on mutually satisfying goals increases the likelihood of success.

Teaching methods are established by considering the various ways that learners learn. Varied methods allow for different learning styles of the learners. Expand the learner's concept of how learning occurs. Share with them how much there is to learn, the sources and opportunities to learn. Let them know that learning can occur in the absence of a teacher. In establishing learning procedures, identify the risks of learning and minimizing those risks. For example, it is risky to share one's thought or ideas. Establish early that no one will be ridiculed for his opinions. If someone is timid about reading Bible names, share with the entire group that many of us do not always know the proper pronunciation.

In establishing any rules or procedures necessary for the learning environment, make sure the rules are clearly stated and understood by class members. These guidelines apply to youth retreats, preschool Sunday School, or senior adult Bible study. These rules may include the way discussion will occur, what is off limits, and the way class business is conducted. Surprises in rules are not motivating. Rules should be seen as objective and applied consistently and justly to all, not at the whim of the teacher. If the learners are genuinely involved in making the rules and establishing the goals and procedures, they will be more motivated toward learning.

Choosing Teaching Methods

Because people learn in many different ways, we must teach with different methods. In fact, the only one "bad" teaching method is the one that is used exclusively, without new ones introduced when needed. Different age groups need different teaching methods.

In teaching preschoolers, we use learning methods that include art activities; dramatic play; nature; books; puzzles; Bible thoughts and verses; games; poetry; homeliving; and pictures. Learning methods for older children include more varied art experiences; creative dramatics; creative writing; music; and discussion activities. Lectures; variations of lecture; brainstorming; question and answers; research; group discussion; small group work; and case studies may be methods used to teach youth and adults. These are not a complete list of all learning methods, but should point to the multiplicity of learning methods that may be used.

Various teaching strategies are appropriate. There is no one magic formula for a guaranteed successful method. The following questions will help you in selecting appropriate teaching methods.

1. What is the nature of the material to be presented? Does the material deal with facts? A survey of the Old and New Testaments may be fact oriented. Is hands-on experience important in what you are studying? Any type of mission study should ideally involve some activity. The nature of the material and the projected outcome determine the best teaching strategy.

2. What methods are appealing to this particular age group? Think

about the age group. What would they like to do? What is fun and challenging?

3. What is the desired outcome of the teaching/learning session? Are you seeking primarily to convey information? Do you want your learner to have an attitude change? Are there certain skills that should be learned? Knowing what you hope to achieve influences the choice of activities or strategies to reach the goal.

4. What strategies are most comfortable for you? While your focus should be primarily upon the learner, your viewpoint is important. If you try a strategy with which you are uncomfortable, you will convey that discomfort to the learner and impair learning. However, being uncomfortable does not excuse you from developing new effective teaching strategies.

Using Teaching Methods to Reach Learning Goals

Good teaching methods relate to learning. Simple enough! As learning goals are identified, specific learning principles help learners reach those goals. Leroy Ford in his work *Design for Teaching and Training* gives an excellent description of the construction of goals and various learning principles that facilitate goal attainment.[2] To help your learning, these principles are given in chart form followed by ways to apply in local church teaching. Teaching for knowledge, understanding, attitudes and values, and motor skills will be described.

Knowledge: ability to repeat facts or recall specific information
What to do in teaching for knowledge:
 involve the learners in active response;
 employ multiple sense usage;
 use advanced organizers to establish direction;
 provide immediate feedback to the learner;
 attempt numerous and varied activities toward the goal; and
 have novel or new activities.[3]

Knowledge forms the basis for much of learning. Knowledge, in our definition, is repeating information. If knowledge is the goal, the teacher may decide to teach the story of the good Samaritan. Various ways to involve the learner's sense would include acting out the story; imagining the smell along the road; describing what an eyewitness saw; and listening to the townspeople relate the story. Active response may include completing a listening guide to the story or searching Scripture for answers to given questions. The teacher may begin the lesson by outlining the major events in the story—using an advanced organizer. As the learners make response throughout the lesson, give feedback of progress. You can use different activities to present the lesson, like telling the story in modern language; writing a newspaper article on the event; or writing future letters between the victim and the good Samaritan. Novel or new activities may include describing a reunion between the victim and the good Samaritan or presenting a case as to why the good Samaritan should be named "Man of the Year." As the reader will quickly discover, these examples overlap each other in learning principles. Furthermore, some of these principles and examples may be used to teach for understanding.

Understanding involves the learner's translating of the knowledge (given information) into more personalized and applied incidences. Various levels or steps in the understanding domain include understanding—paraphrasing information; application—using the information in a specific way; analysis—breaking down material into its various components; synthesis—creating information based upon various parts; and evaluating—judging based upon a given criteria.[4] Step by step, understanding magnifies the importance and usefulness of the information for the learner.

Studying John 3:16 demonstrates the various levels of understanding. If the learner memorizes and repeats John 3:16, he or she demonstrates knowledge. Paraphrasing John 3:16 is an example of understanding. Using John 3:16 in a case study demonstrates application. If the learner breaks down the verse into key elements, he or she would demonstrate analysis. Creating a program that reveals the truth of the verse is an example of synthesis. Learners make an evaluation by judging two mission projects to determine the one that most clearly expresses John 3:16. Each of these examples shows a development of greater understanding in the study of the Scripture passage. The following principles will aid in teaching for understanding.

Understanding: translating knowledge (given information) into more personalized and applied ways.
What to do in teaching for understanding:
    use principles for teaching knowledge;
    translate ideas into new forms;

discover how one idea relates to another;
define or interpret ideas;
apply information in a new situation;
break down material into its parts;
use systematic problem-solving;
combine elements to form a new creative "product"; and
place a value or judgment on something based upon given standards.[5]

Teaching for understanding builds upon knowledge and the principles of teaching knowledge. Have the students translate the knowledge into new forms by making a collage, creating a play, making a model, or writing a story. Ask such questions as why? how does? and what if? as you try to relate one idea to another. Break down material into small parts by outlining a book of the Bible, looking at the truths in Jesus' parables or planning the components of a retreat. Teach problem solving and increase understanding with case studies, counseling problems, and simulation games. Have one group of students design a model for a good Sunday School organization (creating a new product) and have another group evaluate it. Teaching for understanding is exciting and challenging!

Teaching for attitudes and values involves the learner's mind-set toward a specific situation or life in general. Attitudes and values are developed in various stages: receiving—becoming aware that something exists; responding—some small degree of commitment with no action yet; valuing—attaching worth to something with some level of pursuit; organization—bringing several values or attitudes to a given situation with the need to determine its priority; and characterization—a life-style that reflects committed values and attitudes.[6]

Attitudes and Values: mindset toward a specific situation or life in general.
What to do in teaching attitudes and values:
observe leaders and peers who set the example;
read and hear about persons who set the example;
consult sources considered authoritative;
identify the attitude and what it means;
provide meaningful emotional experiences;
provide opportunity for positive action;

practice decision making;
reflect upon life's experiences; and
share insights with others.[7]

Christian teaching develops values and attitudes. Not acquired overnight, values are developed and nurtured over time and involve various experiences. In small, everyday experiences, values are acquired and practiced. These steps move from general awareness to specific application of that value. Ultimately, a life-style commitment emerges that reflects values. For example, to teach your students the values of social responsibility, give examples from books and real life. Invite a social worker to speak. Even better, provide on-the-job experiences like working in a well-baby clinic or a meals-on-wheel program. Let the students come together and recount their experiences, such as books read, people observed, or experiences shared.

Motor skills involve the ability to perform a physical activity with a degree of skill and ease. Steps in developing motor skills include perception—awareness through the sense; set—mental and physical readiness to act; guided response—learner attempts under the guidance of an expert; habit—skills mastered to the point of being habitual; and complex overt response—a complex activity performed with a high degree of skill.[8]

Motor Skills: performing physical activities with a degree of skill and ease.
What to do in teaching motor skills:
   view in advance the skills;
   see a step-by-step demonstration of the skill;
   orally repeat a plan for carrying out the skill;
   guide early attempts in the task;
   repeat skills with little or no guidance; and
   practice under realistic conditions.[9]

Teaching a person to witness, for example, may involve providing the learner with a list of important skills (viewing the skills in advance); watching a film demonstration of a witnessing encounter (demonstration of the skill); repeating the skills (oral recitation); practicing witnessing with a trainer (guided response); and going on a door-to-door visitation program (repeated attempts under realistic conditions).

In an orderly fashion, certain skills important to the Christian life can be taught.

Looking Back

Teaching involves motivating. Motivation must occur in the life of the teacher, the learner, the learning climate, and the teaching methods. All of these areas influence each other. Teaching/learning is motivating.

We are pleased to present you with your completed passport to teaching/learning. You have studied information related to the biblical and historical foundations; elements of a theory of teaching/learning; the role of the learner; the role of the teacher; the lesson plan and its implications; and ways of motivating the learner toward learning. These elements will form the core insights and skills necessary to explore the varied world of Christian teaching/learning.

Looking Ahead

With your passport now acquired, you will now begin to visit a variety of settings in Christian teaching/learning. The passport will allow you to visit and to see the sights and smells of these various locations. In part 2, you will visit selected contexts of teaching/ learning: the Sunday School or Bible teaching program; the worship service; leadership training; missions education; study groups; committees; mission activities; music; and writing. Your first stop is Sunday School or the Bible teaching program.

Notes

1. Robert C. Hawley, "Perspectives On Motivation," *Teacher* 91 (October 1973): 43-45.

2. See Leroy Ford, *Design for Teaching and Training: A Self Study Guide to Lesson Planning* (Nashville: Broadman, 1978).

3. Ford, 118.

4. See Benjamin S. Bloom, ed. *Taxonomy of Educational Objectives, Handbook I: Cognitive Domain* (New York: David McKay, 1956).

5. Ford, 163; 195.

6. See David R. Krathwohl, Benjamin S. Bloom, and Bertram B. Marsia, *Taxonomy of Educational Objectives, Handbook II: Affective Domain* (New York: David McKay, 1964).

7. Ford, 225; 242.

8. See Elizabeth Simpson, *Taxonomy of Psychomotor Domain* (Unpublished paper), Urbana: University of Illinois, 1968.

9. Ford, 292.

Learning Activities

1. Teacher Motivation

A. List the five ways described for the teacher to be motivated. Provide three examples of how each might be implemented.

B. If you are a teacher, describe how you go about "motivating yourself." If you are not a teacher, discuss with a teacher how he "motivates himself."

C. Imagine that you have been given ten minutes to prepare a motivational talk for church teachers. What would be the key elements that you would describe? Explain.

D. What are additional ways that help motivate teachers?

2. Motivational Climate

A. In your opinion, what are the key ingredients in an effective motivational climate for learning?

B. Create a mural that depicts the right "motivational climate" for learning.

C. Compare and contrast qualities in a poor motivational climate with those in a good motivational climate.

3. Learner Motivation

A. Identify ways that teachers can seek to increase the motivation among their learners.

B. Think of a quality teacher that you have experienced. What did the teacher do to motivate the class? What did the teacher do to motivate you personally?

C. Think of a poor teacher that you have experienced. What did the teacher do to motivate the class? What did the teacher do to motivate you personally?

D. What role does the learner play in his own motivation?

E. What is the relationship between motivation and age? What are the implications, if any, for the teacher?

4. Learning Methods

A. Select any age group. List learning methods that are appropriate for that age group.

B. What is the relationship between learning methods and teaching strategies? Explain.

C. What learning methods are most appealing to you? Do these methods have any impact upon how you teach?

D. Create a poster that shows how to select an appropriate learning method.

5. Learning Methods Related to Teaching Goals

A. What is the relationship between learning methods and teaching goals? Explain.

B. List principles involved in teaching for knowledge. Choose an example and illustrate how to use these principles.

C. Draw a picture depicting the various steps in understanding. Beside each step give an example.

D. List principles involved in teaching for understanding. Choose an example and illustrate how to use these principles.

E. Draw a picture to illustrate the various steps in attitudes and values.

F. List principles involved in teaching for attitudes and values. Choose an example and illustrate how to use these principles.

G. Draw a series of cartoons to illustrate the steps involved in acquiring a skill.

H. Choose a skill to be taught. Illustrate with the learning principles how to teach that skill.

PART II | **The World of Christian Teaching/Learning**
or
The When and Where of Christian Teaching/Learning

7. | Sunday School or Bible Teaching Program

Establishing Importance

It's as American as homemade apple pie, hand-churned ice cream, and roast beef for Sunday dinner. The Sunday School or the Bible teaching program of the local church is a unique expression of American Protestantism. Entire families, ranging from young babies to aging adults, going to church on Sunday morning for Bible study is a familiar occurrence in most communities. Today, the Sunday School is an established institution of American culture. However, this acceptance has not always been true.

In its beginning in the eighteenth century, the Sunday School was not warmly received by American churches.[1] In fact, some early pastors regarded the Sunday School as something less than Christian because of its meeting on the Lord's Day. Despite this initial cold reception from the church, the Sunday School movement began to flourish through the efforts of interested laypeople.

These lay groups sponsored the development of Sunday Schools throughout the growing United States. Often the Sunday School was the only place of educational instruction in some isolated communities. Included in the Sunday School was the teaching of reading. Soon these early Sunday School societies began publishing their own literature. In many instances, these early Sunday Schools were the primary places of both moral and educational instruction in the community.

Beginning in the mid-nineteenth century, various churches and denominations adopted the goals of the Sunday School. Denominations established their own Sunday Schools in keeping with their own sectarian (denominational) views. By the last quarter of the nineteenth century, the Sunday School had become a vital part of American culture.

The Sunday School or the Bible teaching program is the primary teaching/learning avenue of most churches. Apart from what occurs during the worship service, the Sunday School may be the only place where individuals receive formal instruction in Christian teachings. To keep the church strong, the teaching program must be kept strong, vital, and growing. Strong growing churches have long been associated with strong Bible teaching programs.

Defining Chapter Goals

You will now explore the teaching context of the Sunday School. The following guidelines will strengthen the church's primary teaching/learning program. At the conclusion of this chapter the learner should be able to do the following:

- describe ways of making the Sunday School a total teaching program;
- identify ways to improve worker involvement;
- describe the importance of organizing for effective learning;
- defend the importance of keeping the Bible primary in Sunday School;
- describe specific ways of teaching preschoolers for maximum learning;
- describe specific ways of teaching children for maximum learning;
- describe specific ways of teaching youth for maximum learning;
- describe specific ways of teaching adults for maximum learning; and
- identify specific resources for Sunday School work.

Overall Program Organization

Total Teaching Program

Today's children watch on the average of twenty-five hours of television a week. The average adolescent will have watched 20,000 hours of television at the time of his high school graduation.[2] Compared to the amount of time spent in the public schools and watching the television, the amount of time spent in Sunday School is minimal. The entire experience lasts an hour or less. However, actual Bible study time in that program may be twenty minutes or less, depending upon the utilization of time and resources.

Because of this scarcity of time and other significant outside influences, every minute of the allotted Sunday School time is precious. Moments wasted are moments that cannot be reclaimed. Is an hour too much to devote to the study of the Book of Life? If not, concentrated efforts must be used to maximize that one hour.

Begin the teaching/learning experience at the appointed time. One of the great problems in Sunday School work is starting on time. Many Sunday School departments or classes begin thirty minutes later than their designated times. With such a late start, valuable instruction time is lost forever.

Attending Sunday School on time is like attending any other experience. The same individual who would not arrive at work late is one who may habitually attend Sunday School fifteen or twenty minutes late. We would not send our children late to public school, but we send them late to Sunday School. While we may pride ourselves on our discipline in getting many things accomplished during the week, we forget the importance of discipline on Sunday morning.

Of all the days of the week, we cannot afford to forget discipline on the Lord's Day. Without hesitation, a strong relationship exists between discipline and discipleship. Starting on time is a first step toward the discipleship process. How does one change a group notorious for not starting on time? The following ideas may be helpful.

Begin with ourselves—As leaders, whether it be as class teacher, department director, outreach leader, or secretary, we have a built-in responsibility to set the example for the department and class. We cannot expect the class members to exceed the faithfulness and discipline that we model week-by-week.

Agreeing to be a leader involves certain basic requirements, such as being on time. For a leader to be on time, he may need to be early. Being early allows for the early-arriving guests and the extra time needed for interruptions. If the teacher doesn't start on time, the class never will. With even a few faithful workers and members present, we should start on time. Gradually, the importance of starting on time will become evident. It may involve several months; however, if we don't begin the practice of starting on time, we will never start on time.

Offer meaningful activities from the beginning—Something meaningful should occur from the time the persons enter the department until they depart for the worship service. Time is too precious to relinquish to quiet abandonment. The first moments may be spent in greeting and fellowship. This is an important ingredient in a successful Sunday School. However, do not let the lingering and greeting extend for the next thirty minutes.

In departmental periods, a planned devotional or some other type of presentation is essential. Failure to plan teaches a significant message. Why should I bother to get there on time if there is no reason? Work at making your programming so good that people will want to be present. Poor departmental planning is often associated with poor attendance and poor starting time.

Honor the ending time—While we have focused on the importance of starting on time, additional words are needed about ending on time. The ending is just as important as the beginning. Conclude the Sunday School session in a meaningful manner. Exciting ways to end the lesson include summarizing the day's activities; encouraging attendance next Sunday; planning for specific activities of ministry and Christian growth; and encouraging those present to attend the worship service.

End the Bible teaching hour on schedule. Do not hold a captive audience. Even though some were late in attending, don't get even now by holding them back. Honor the structure by giving them ample time to do whatever preparations are necessary for worship. We live up to the standards set before us, as well as the structure set before us. By making the Sunday School a total teaching period with quality instruction, we set before others a quality example to follow.

Involve All Workers—Historically, the "earthly" success of Sunday School has been its lay emphasis. The effective Sunday School is comprised of many dedicated workers, beyond that of the teacher. All workers, such as the greeters, secretaries, music/song leaders, are needed to participate fully throughout the Bible teaching program. After people have been greeted, visitors directed to the respective classes, and records have been returned, what happens to certain workers? Some disappear to the church kitchen for coffee and others visit in the hallways. These types of behaviors displayed week after week teach a powerful lesson to other Sunday School members—Sunday School is not that important. "I have done my part. I'm through until same time next week."

Workers who accept responsibilities in Sunday School must be prepared and willing to carry out those commitments on a week-by-week basis. Faithful workers produce faithful Sunday School members. In addition, new Sunday School workers have their impressions of "how to do the job" by associating with other workers. By our work in Sunday School, we model not only for the Sunday School member but also for the Sunday School worker.

Best Teaching Organization

How do you grade a Sunday School? Grading does not mean giving an A, B, or C to the organization. Grading means organizing the people into workable and teachable units. Various theories exist regarding the best organizational plan for Sunday Schools. As a general rule, grouping does not seem to pose a serious problem until the adult years. Prior to the adult years, grouping is generally based upon the school grade. Without the guideline of a school grade, what becomes the basis for the adult organization?

One of the best ways to organize adults is by a common age range. While this plan is not without criticism, it may be the best solution to a difficult problem. Generally, people in a given age group are experiencing the same developmental tasks, such as getting married, beginning a job, rearing children, caring for parents, or planning for retirement. There is common ground for interests and concerns. This commonality builds class fellowship, as well as mutual learning. If age grading is used, each church must decide upon the best age ranges for its own current situation, as well as its potential for growth.

Another issue in organization is the size of the class and the class enrollment. One view argues that there should be no limit upon the number enrolled and the number attending a given class. In fact, the attendance is limited only by the seating capacity of the available space. For example, a hundred people may be taught by one teacher. I have seen this view practiced throughout the various ages of the church members.

An opposing view centers around a growth orientation that stresses both moderate enrollments and class size. Generally expected class attendance follows fifty per cent of enrollment. For example, if thirty are enrolled, on any given Sunday the average attendance is fifteen. A growth-oriented approach stresses limits on enrollments in both departments and individual classes. A good class size is approximately ten to twelve in attendance where everyone contributes to the functioning of the class. Enrollment in class may be limited to approximately twenty-five. When numbers exceed twenty-five enrolled, new units or classes are started. These newly formed classes will also grow to their maximum capacity.

Smaller units allow for greater learner participation and the training of more teachers. In churches, there are two levels of education occurring. One level stresses education for the members; another level stresses education for the leaders. If there is a group of one hundred enrolled with one teacher, only one teacher is preparing the lesson. If there are four groups with four teachers, four teachers are preparing the lesson. Personal growth occurs as teachers prepare. More classes allow for the training of more leaders.

Organization should also allow for flow within the Sunday School groups. Healthy groups tend to have members moving in and out of the group. Members may move to other groups as they get older; members may move on to other leadership roles. New members should be continually brought into the group. Through visitation, ministry, and quality teaching, this growth should be a natural occurrence. Groups that tend to remain the same year after year generally are limited in growth potential. These groups often become closed not only to "outsiders" but also to enhanced growth and maturity.

Bible-Based Program

While it may sound ridiculous to stress the importance of keeping the Bible as the focus of the teaching/learning, some churches have abandoned the Bible for other studies, such as books on spiritual life, philosophy, or biography. While all of these studies may be worthwhile, this choice is not the choice for Sunday School.

The Sunday School must keep the Bible as its central task in its teaching/learning. Commentaries and other resources may be used. However, the Bible is primary. To focus away from the Bible is to abandon the Book that provides ultimate meaning and direction to all. Sunday Schools that fail are those who abandon the living Word for other substitutes.

While the above guidelines form the basis for all Sunday Schools, distinctives exist between the various age groupings in Sunday School.

Remember, the person is our primary focus. It is impossible to provide all that is needed in working with specific age groups. Such information is beyond the scope of this work. However, summary information may help in beginning specialized age-group work in Sunday School. Please note that many of the designated concepts will apply to more than one age group.

Preschool Work

"Working with preschool? Don't you mean babysitting?" the would-be teacher responded. Unfortunately, that attitude reflects a grave misunderstanding. Often preschoolers are the victims of poor teaching because of ignorance on the part of teachers and other workers. Preschoolers are definitely capable of learning. In fact, the preschool child will learn in spite of poor teaching. To learn is a natural part of the child's make-up. The following key concepts will describe some unique and important aspects of the teaching/learning process for preschoolers. Focusing on and magnifying these elements can lead to quality teaching/learning.

Relationships

While relationships are important to all teaching/learning, relationships have special significance for this age. Relationships formed here will influence future relationships. Noted psychologist Eric Erickson has identified various stages through which young children move. Each of these stages is a crisis that will be resolved either positively or negatively. These crises include trust versus mistrust; autonomy versus doubt; and guilt versus initiative. The primary resolution of each of these crises will depend upon the quality of relationship between the child and his primary caregivers and other significant individuals.

Although what happens during the week may be beyond the church's control, we can assume responsibility for the child while in our church care. An opportunity is created for the teaching of relationships. As relationships among the child and his teachers and other children are emphasized, the foundations for future relationships with God are established. Either positively or negatively, the child's attitudes toward the church and God are shaped by these early relationships.

Relationships formed may hinder or foster all future teaching/learning experiences. Ways of positively fostering this potential learning include establishing trust for the teacher and classroom; providing security for the preschoolers; demonstrating Christlike concern for all; fostering self-respect for each; establishing guidelines for acceptable behavior; and balancing growing independence needs and dependence needs. These principles, translated both into attitudes and concrete activities, provide the foundations upon which future teaching/learning occur.

Thematic Activity

Activity for preschoolers is important. With short attention spans and active motor skills, these children must be involved in activity. However, these activities should be based upon some type of concept or theme. A concept or theme is an idea that guides the teaching/learning content. Identifying and focusing upon a basic theme can enhance the meaningfulness of the individual teaching/learning experience for the child. These themes may include friendship, cooperation, the family, God, self and helping.

Let the planned activities illustrate the basic theme of the lesson. Activities used by perceptive teachers may become teachable moments for the young child. For example, in building a house, the teacher may quietly talk about how God seeks to provide homes for us. "Homes are good. We should take care of our homes. How can we take care of our homes?" Such an activity, both planned and unplanned, is a thematic activity rather than just "playing with the blocks." Great themes of life are learned, rehearsed, and practiced in everyday activities.

Flexible and Adaptable Schedule

The best constructed plans may need to be altered in light of individual need. With short attention spans and other pressing concerns, the teacher must be flexible and adaptable in what is done. In fact, the wise teacher will have more activities planned than can be accomplished in the session. Thus, activity may be changed in light of number of students, mood level, and interest level. Better to have too many possible activities than too few. Too few activities may lead to boredom and misbehavior. Quality planning allows for the unexpected.

Repetition

Children learn through repetition. While the repetition may bore us as adults, it provides reinforcement for the child. Children enjoy doing and learning through repeated activity. Repeatedly singing a song or playing a Bible game can be delightful to the young child as well as a reinforcement to learning. Look into the eyes of the child, examine the expressions on his face, and listen to his voice. Here you will discover the importance of repeating. Here you will learn the importance of varying the repetition.

Repeat activities with variety. One of my favorite teachers related how she guided children in drawing circles. Soon the children grew tired of drawing circles. She said, "Okay, lets draw cookies." Later they drew wheels or rings. The same task was accomplished—drawing circles—but with interest, imagination, and inventiveness. Use that principle in working with children. Sing "Jesus Loves Me" in a variety of ways such as having the children sit down, having the children stand up, having the girls sing one stanza and the boys the next, and having the children walk around the room. Let variety and imagination inspire your use of repetition.

Atmosphere

The atmosphere in teaching preschoolers is important. Brightly colored and well-kept rooms will enhance the teaching/learning experience. In addition, the atmosphere must include workers who are present. Arriving early is important for those who work with preschoolers and children. Often parents of preschoolers are teachers themselves in other areas. If an adult is not present to take care of their child, these parents are hindered in getting to their own classroom. The whole system may be disrupted. Arriving early and preparing an atmosphere ready for early arriving preschoolers is crucial. Remember, this hour in Sunday School may be the preschoolers' one hour of love, acceptance, and godly instruction for the entire week. Keep the atmosphere that important. Work toward the child's wanting to return next week to Sunday School.

Sense Experience

Provide as many varied sense experiences as possible for the preschooler. The greater the sense experience, the greater the teaching/ learning possibilities. Let the teaching/learning involve various sight, sound, taste, and touch experiences. Select a theme and plan various activities that will involve as many as possible of the child's senses as each sense reinforces the teaching/ learning experience. Vary the activities in order to utilize all the sense potentialities of the young child.

Children's Work

Guiding the teaching/learning of children becomes more challenging as they exhibit more and more of their innate intellectual capacity and more and more of their desire for independence. The child's world is vastly expanding. In fact, home is gradually replaced by the broader world of school and play. The church must compete with other attractions. Field trips to the zoo and museum; hours spent in computer-based instruction and more hours spent in computer-based games; time on athletic fields; hours spent in music, drama, art, and dance lessons; these are the worlds of children. What was appealing to a preschooler may no longer be quite as appealing to a school-age child. The following guidelines may help in the teaching of children.

Learning to Choose

Working with children becomes an opportunity for allowing them to make more and more of their own choices. Initially the freedom to choose may be more limited; with increasing age, choices become less limited. Because children need experience in making wise choices, the church has a unique opportunity in developing this ability.

Allow the child to choose among various alternatives in learning activities or projects. One child may choose to make a poster; another may create a newspaper; still another may make a Bible mobile. Help them to see what is involved in their choices. Once the choice is made, guide them in completing the choice. Learning to accept responsibility and to follow through on choices is important. With increased experience, the child will learn to choose with wisdom and "stick-to-itiveness."

Increasing Skill Activity

Throughout the school years, the child is acquiring more developed skills in such areas as reading, writing, and arithmetic. Utilization of these developing verbal skills is a primary way for the teacher to teach. Allowing the child to read aloud Scripture, to read silently and follow directions, to tell a story, to play a game, and to write are significant learning accomplishments for this child. In search of praise, children naturally look forward to showing and sharing what they can do. Match the learning activities with the skills of the child. Be careful not to embarrass the child who may be deficient in some of these skills. Let all be praised for the skills they possess.

Planning for Success

Not every child is successful with the experiences found in schools. Lack of school success can lead to frustration. Children who are not successful in school tend to drop out of school. These children tend to pursue other activities, not always healthy, in order to achieve some measure of success.

Perceived success is an important ingredient in developing a healthy self-concept. The church's teaching/learning opportunities can provide reinforcement for the worth of the child and his growing self-esteem. Plan Bible-learning activities in which all children will be successful. While each child may achieve a different level of success, each child needs some measure of success. Without some success experience, the child is more apt to "drop out," becoming indifferent to the efforts and teachings of the church.

Focusing on Increasing Application

As children grow older, they have more and more capacity to apply biblical truths to their daily lives. These children need to be challenged in specific ways to transfer what is learned in Sunday School to their lives beyond the confines of the church. In the selection of learning activities, give children opportunity to practice what they have learned. Make the learning meaningful to their everyday experiences. Use games, role playing, and discussion groups as avenues for increasing application of biblical truths.

Communicating Through Relationships

Children are experiencing a world with varied influences. Our culture is pluralistic—many philosophies, interests, values, and ideas. Regardless of how we try to protect and guide our children, they are influenced by these factors. Children need to be able to communicate these discoveries with others. Christian teachers can provide the needed listening ears.

Children need a chance to talk about what is going on in their world. Many of our problems, both as children and adults, could be avoided if we had opportunities to express our feelings, questions, and ideas. Failure to communicate effectively with this age group will diminish the communication possibilities with them as they reach adolescence. The teacher must establish a relationship that allows the child to trust and to communicate his joys, as well as sorrows. Communication patterns set during this age will influence subsequent development in the life changes of adolescence.

Youth Work

Not only do adolescents undergo rapid changes with their physical bodies but also with their mental and social lives. These changes highly influence their religious growth and development. In this stage the adolescent begins to ask questions like the scientist. While answers may have been readily accepted without question or scrutiny, now everything seems to be questioned. No questions today, but tomorrow everything is questioned. Highly idealistic, these adolescents are prone to be disillusioned as Christian leaders and the church fail to live up to the adolescents' high expectations. Once disillusioned, the youth may withdraw from the church.

Socially, this age group is trying desperately to find a group with which to identify. Identification is desired; social bonds are necessary. Adolescents will be attracted to those groups where they feel accepted and where they can accept the group's ideology. Isolated adolescents are especially vulnerable to the teaching of various religious cults. Sexually, this group is trying to discover and to practice its own sexual identity. Changes in their bodies create psychological tension that must be resolved as they continue in the formulation of their own identity. Feelings of sexuality may be difficult to accept depending upon their Christian upbringing. Firmly established moral teachings are needed.

Vocationally, the adolescent is trying to discover how he fits in with the rest of the world. What should he do with his life? In the ever-changing world of the adolescent, choices regarding the will of God are significant. The following guidelines may be helpful in guiding youth in Christian teaching/learning opportunities.

Challenge Youth Intellectually

Youth have the ability to think inquisitively and critically. Help them to use these skills in their Bible study. Guide them in learning how to interpret the Bible. Help them begin to see the relevancy of Scripture for daily life and practice. Teaching/learning opportunities must meet these growing intellectual abilities. Work with adolescents as they use their minds to explore God's Word and His world.

Design Wholesome Fellowship Opportunities

Be sensitive to helping youth find acceptance in the church. Youth need healthy opportunities for experiencing and developing relationships with the same and opposite sex. Regardless of how indifferent they may appear, either physically or verbally, youth need to feel a part of the church body. If not, they will seek affiliation with other groups that will satisfy this urgent need for fellowship. Plan activities that will meet their needs for socializing with themselves, as well as with other age groups in church.

Provide Appropriate Male and Female Sex Roles

Crucial to adolescents is the role modeling provided by contact with both male and female teachers. Often it may be difficult to find males willing to teach or lead in this age group. However, a powerful message is presented if males are not a part of the Sunday School programming for adolescents. Sunday School may become regarded as simply an activity for females. Role models help in learning, as well as in choosing an appropriate mate for later life.

Engage in Active Listening

The plan of the teaching/learning sessions must illustrate increasing attention to the concerns and the questions raised by adolescents. The many and varied questions that are in their minds need to be addressed in the context of genuine concern and truth. Active listening will increase the relationship between the adolescent and her church. Should the church fail to listen to the adolescent, the adolescent may in turn fail to listen to the church and its teachings. Open hearts and open ears establish quality relationships.

Discover the Will of God

This age group faces many significant questions. These questions to a great extent will involve the ability to discover and to follow God's leadership. Adolescents need the ability to know how to find God's will in such areas of their life as sexuality, vocation, peer relationships, and school.

Helping to provide the tools throughout the teaching/learning process will greatly aid this discovery. Help them to know how to use the resources of Scripture, the counsel of wise Christians, the power of prayer, and genuine self-examination. Helping adolescents discern for themselves will produce more mature individuals who are capable of "rightly explaining the word of truth" (2 Tim. 2:15).

Integrate Faith and Learning

This age group is bombarded with various challenges to their Christian faith. Technology and other educational pursuits confront and challenge their belief system. Ideas range from "there is no God" to "you are a god." Adolescents need the tools and the reassurance to know that God is the author of all truth.

All of life, including academic study, vocational pursuits, and personal relationships, should be infused with Christian faith. Faith should complement every aspect of life. We should not compartmentalize our lives into a "real" life and a "religious" life. Adolescents can learn this lesson if they know about and associate with adults who have made such a reality of their own lives. As they pursue higher education, adolescents need the ability to take their faith into all areas of study. As they leave for further schooling or for the job market, make sure they have the opportunity to know that God is alive and interested in what they do and what they study. Let faith and learning, as well as faith and life, go hand-in-hand with the adolescent's approach into the adult world.

Adult Work

The world of the adult and the world of the adolescent are vastly different. The adult no longer has the luxury of discussing philosophical ideas within the security of parental care. The adult must learn to balance the check book, mow the lawn, hold down a job, and keep up with his laundry. Life concerns become more pragmatic and practical. The adult has varying responsibilities resting, sometimes burdening, upon his shoulders.

Similar to adolescents, adults are still subject to pressures of finding their identity and confronting peer pressure. In young adulthood, there is a tremendous pressure to establish relationships and to achieve such success as having a family, a nice home, automobiles, and luxurious vacations. In middle adulthood, there is the crisis of recognizing one's own mortality as life changes. Remaining a youth is not possible. In senior adulthood, the adult must discover ways that he can still make meaningful contributions to life. The following guidelines may provide insight in working with adults in Sunday School.

Using Adult Knowledge and Experience

The adult has a wide range of experiences in business, raising a family, and managing a budget. A successful teaching/learning situation allows the adult to share from his experience and knowledge. Adults want to participate in the choosing of study content. Because of an adult's own experiences, he may challenge the teacher. The successful teacher is willing to work nondefensively with the adult and to learn from him. Adults learn together through mutual participation.

Focusing on Adult Life Concerns

Because of various time and energy demands placed upon them, adults are interested in studying what has practical value for them. Here the teacher must show the usefulness and the practicality of the Christian faith. What does the Bible have to contribute regarding the daily concerns and problems of the adults? These principles can include diverse, yet highly personal, items.

When my employment may be in jeopardy, how can I act ethically at work? What is the correct way to parent my children? What is my responsibility toward my aging parents as well as my own family? How can I live with disappointments? How can I accept my own mortality? Good participation and attendance should occur in a class when the teacher who can relate biblical truth with the adult's life concerns.

Encouraging and Assuming Responsibility

Adults need to be confronted with their relationship and responsibility to the church as a whole. To a degree, through adolescence, the individual has been on the receiving end of the church. Now he has increased opportunity and ability to give more to the overall functioning of the church. Regardless of age, there are ministry opportunities that exist. Every life has a participatory role to fulfill in church. Sunday School work should encourage adult participation in the community of faith.

Ministering to Various Identity Crises

Each man and woman experiences various identity crises throughout life, and teachers need to be sensitive to these. Crises are not damaging in themselves. Crises offer an opportunity either to grow as a Christian or to stagnate or regress.

The young adult's crisis may be a lack of satisfaction with his job or profession. He may feel that he is going nowhere and has nowhere to turn. The middle-aged adult may recognize his vanishing youth. Attempts that may be made to recapture youth may be either healthy or nonhealthy. In senior adulthood, the adult must come to grips with certain ambitions that will never be realized.

These various crisis points should be addressed periodically by the teachers of adults. Biblical instruction can give direction and comfort in meeting these crossroads in life. Christian living can be enhanced through the resolution of these times of change.

Allowing for Choice and Direction

Teaching adults involves allowing adults to make choices regarding their study. Their preferences should be acknowledged and sought. By making adults feel they have a choice, you increase their own faithfulness in achieving the established goals. The goals of the class become more personal and more likely to be attained. Teaching/learning is enhanced if adults are given responsibility for choice and direction. In fact, it is a part of the making or maturing of disciples.

Reviewing the Opportunity

The above discussion provides insight into the special nature of various age groups within the Sunday School setting. However, this information can be applied to any specialized learning setting. The identified distinctives can apply to many situations and individuals. The teaching/learning process is a cumulative one, built upon knowledge of the person, the aims of the organizations, and the work of the teacher. The better we can know people and their concerns and the more we address these concerns, the greater our teaching effectiveness.

Notes

1. For further study on the Sunday School, see Robert W. Lynn and Elliott Wright, *Big Little School: Two Hundred Years of Sunday School*, 2d ed. (Religious Education Press, 1980).

2. John W. Santrock, *Adolescence*, 4th ed. (Wm. C. Brown Publishers, 1990), 350-1.

The following books may be helpful in teaching/learning through the Sunday School.

Dunn, Frank E. *The Ministering Teacher*. Judson, 1982.

Hall, Terry. *How to Be the Best Sunday School Teacher You Can Be.* Moody, 1986.

Johnson, Kent L. *Called to Teach: Ideas & Encouragement for Teachers in the Church.* Augsburg Fortress, 1984.

Krych, Margaret A. *Teaching The Gospel Today: A Guide for Education in the Congregation.* Augsburg Fortress, 1987.

Malehor, Harold A. *Over Two Hundred Ways to Improve Your Sunday School.* Concordia, 1982.

Swain, Dorothy G. *Teach Me To Teach.* Judson, 1964.

Taulman, James. *Encouragers: The Sunday School Worker's Counseling Ministry.* Broadman, 1986.

——— *Help! I Need an Idea.* Broadman, 1987.

Towns, Elmer L. *One Hundred Fifty Four Steps to Revitalize Your Sunday School.* Victor, 1988.

8. | The Worship Service

Worship
Service

Establishing Importance

One of the church's most overlooked teaching/learning opportunities is its worship service. In a single gathering, large numbers of people are brought together. Many regular going church members have difficulty finding a seat twice a year—Christmas and Easter. At Easter, one minister said that he wanted to be the first to say "Merry Christmas." His remark implied that it would be December before he would see many members of the congregation again. The worship service is the only experience that some individuals have with church and formal Christian teaching. It has value even if it is only twice a year for some.

Worship derives from the Anglo Saxon words for "worth" and "ship."[1] Worship involves granting a condition of worth to God. Different types and styles of worship exist. While objective worship is directed exclusively toward God, subjective worship focuses upon the current needs, concerns, and interests of the congregation. Although worship has various functions, the teaching aspects of worship will be examined.

Defining Chapter Goals

At the conclusion of this chapter, the learner should be able to do the following:

- analyze a worship service in light of structure, participation, components, goals, and outcome;
- identify six guidelines for improving the teaching aspects of worship;
- list six common mistakes made in children's sermons;
- list six guidelines for planning the children's sermon; and
- identify resources to assistant in planning worship services and children's sermons.

An Analysis of a Worship Service

Structure

Imagine yourself in your regular place of worship. Look around the room, noticing its various elements. What do the structure and elements teach? For example, does your place of worship have costly chandeliers and expensive stained glass? If so, what do these artifacts contribute to worship? Expensive ornaments may have both positive and negative aspects. They are positive if they focus attention upon the worship and majesty of God. However, the ornaments may hinder worship if we focus upon the beauty of the ornaments and not the Creator God. Worship is also hindered if we fail to look beyond our own church walls to the hurts of people both within and outside the church. Our worship structure conveys a message.

In many Protestant churches, the pulpit is the center from which the Word of God is proclaimed. The Word of God is taught both literally and symbolically through the pulpit's physical placement. Behind the pulpit often there is a baptistry, symbolizing the importance of baptism and the public profession of the Christian life. In front of the pulpit is the Lord's Supper table which illustrates the importance of the communion with God and other believers by remembering Christ's sacrificial death.

These structures teach a basic message. While we may not think about the message on a conscious level, it nevertheless teaches a message. As a young teen, I asked my pastor why we had freshly cut flowers every Sunday morning. Being ecologically and economically minded, I thought it would be cheaper to have artificial flowers that could be reused every Sunday. My minister said the cut flowers symbolized our fresh approach and desire to worship our living God. Fresh flowers were a sign of both respect and joy. His response taught me that worship must be fresh and alive.

Places of worship where there is little care for its physical appearance may indicate indifference. While the congregation may not intend this message, the message may nevertheless be conveyed. The structural atmosphere of worship teaches a basic message to individuals both in and out of the congregation.

Participation

How individuals participate in the worship service teaches a specific message. If there is one primary leader, such as the preacher who does everything, the focus is upon the role of the preacher. This practice may give the impression that the one leader is all powerful and all important to the worship service. No one else may be important. If we don't have the preacher, can we have worship?

Varied participation by all members of the congregation gives the message of unity and interdependence. Participation by all ages and both sexes gives the message that God's family involves everyone. While each group may have different roles of participation, each can participate. Mutual participation encourages worship and learning.

Components

If you are planning a meal or choosing items from a cafeteria line, you are making choices about foods you consider important, essential, or just plain good-tasting. The same idea is true for planning a worship service. The various elements in the worship service teach what we consider to be most important. While some churches maintain the same order of worship each Sunday, other churches have less rigid styles of order. Often there is the goal of achieving a balance between tradition that provides security and change that allows for new life and insight.

The worship elements themselves teach what we consider significant. Examples include the role of announcements, singing, special music, preaching, offering, prayer, and confession. These are elements traditionally found in worship. What we know of worship is often learned by watching these various elements.

Goals

Goals, at first, may seem inappropriate in discussing a worship service. However, goals are present whether verbally expressed or silently understood. What are the expectations of the participants in the worship services? Does the congregation expect anything to happen? If not, chances are nothing will happen to them. Should something happen, they may not be in a position to recognize its existence. Do the leaders expect something to happen? Expectations and goals are often related in the worship service. What we expect becomes our goal; activities and elements are directed toward its end.

Lesson planning has elements common with planning a worship service. In both, we plan to the best of our abilities and pray that God will work in individual lives. In planning a worship service, what is the major focus or intent? As in lesson planning, those responsible for planning a worship service may become frustrated if they fail to identify clearly what are their expectations or hopes for that particular service. Too many individuals may attend church out of habit; too many worship services are planned out of habit. Acting and planning habitually does not promote new growth and direction.

Outcome

What is the outcome or end-result of a religious worship service? What happens in individual lives as a result of having been a participant in worship? Ideally, worship should result in more holy living outside of the place of worship. How are people greeted who make a response during the invitation time? Are they warmly greeted or politely ignored? What behavior does the congregation display to guests? Are the guests made to feel welcome and a part of the worship fellowship? Are people activated for future service? Do people leave with a sense of direction and purpose for the coming week? Do people leave with unmet needs?

Some type of outcome exists from participating in any worship service. What worship outcomes have you observed?

Improving the Teaching Aspects of Worship

Various principles may assist in strengthening the teaching aspects of the worship service. While these suggestions in no way seek to reemphasize "the mystical" or "spiritual" quality of worship, these suggestions can provide a greater unity and emphasis in the services themselves. Unless the Holy Spirit guides, all is in vain.

Identify and Develop the Theme

Identifying the theme is an important consideration in worship. Let the whole service revolve around the message. For example, the selection of the congregational singing, the choice of special music, and the children's sermon can contribute and build toward the minister's message. If the theme is the majesty of God, select the Scriptures, the music, and testimony that will focus, illustrate, and emphasize that theme.

Identifying the theme is not easy. Such identification requires advanced joint preparation by the pastor and the other individuals responsible for planning the service. However, if the service revolves around the theme, the impact of repetition and reinforcement will aid the congregation in learning and practicing the message.

Orderly and coherently, the elements should build and strengthen each other as the service progresses. The end of the worship, like its beginning and development, should continue with that theme. The selection of the closing hymn, the parting prayer, or the week's challenge should summarize and inspire the congregation for the task ahead.

Strive for Unity

Examine the various aspects of the worship service. Do these elements flow together smoothly? The prayer, the songs, the offering, and the message—do they appear graceful? Do certain parts of the service seem rough and choppy? In the sequences of various elements is there coherence? Does each aspect move toward one end?

Use Appropriate and Understandable Language

Language selection is important in all aspects of worship. Language is not an enemy to be deciphered. Instead, language is a medium which communicates and links human beings with one another and with God.

Hymns should be chosen that are understandable. If they are not understandable, it is appropriate to pause and to explain the meaning and the illustrations used in a hymn. Explain the biblical reference in the hymn or the meaning of special words. Singing can be both educational and inspirational!

The language of the sermon should be one that communicates God's truth in ways understandable to the congregation. The sermon is not the time for the minister to impress the congregation with his extensive vocabulary and training. Sermons aimed beyond the thinking level of the congregation are often ignored or misunderstood.

One way to improve the language of the sermon is to use illustrations that call attention to various principles or points of the message. These illustrations should be colorful, attractive, and related directly to the basic content of the message. Using understandable language enhances the teaching potentials of the worship service.

Use Appropriate Printed Information

Printed information can greatly enhance the learning of the congregation. An order of worship can provide a basic framework or guide for the congregation of what will occur in the worship service. Rather than detract from the experience, a well-planned order of worship can focus, direct, and prepare the congregation for enriching experiences.

The printed order of worship can provide information regarding various activities, meetings, and other needs of the congregation and the community. It may include an outline of the basic message. Here the congregation may have opportunity to write down their own comments, insights, and applications. Writing down comments increases the possibility of future retention, reflection, and growth.

Give Reference to Sunday School

Often much is lost from the time people leave Sunday School and enter the worship service. The worship service does provide an opportunity to reinforce and re-illustrate the material studied in Sunday School. This reference can be made in any number of ways. For example, the pastor may refer in his sermon to the ideas studied in the Sunday School lessons if appropriate. Brief comments about the lesson may be made before the singing of an appropriate hymn or the presentation of the special music. In a tangible way, teaching/learning proceses may be reinforced by reminding the congregation of what happened in Sunday School and its importance to the worship service. Non-Sunday School attenders may be encouraged to join in next Sunday's Bible Study.

Involve Active Participation of the People and Their Gifts

Involving various members of the congregation emphasizes the community of God. Having a variety of participation vividly portrays the importance of all individuals in the life and work of God's Kingdom.

All gifts have an opportunity to be shared within the Body of Christ. Giftedness is not something to be hidden and stored but something to be revealed and shared. Active involvement includes the use of drama, such as monologue or play; the use of music; or giving a testimony. By actively participating in using the gifts, we symbolize that God's redemption is vital to all; the life of all is important to the Body. As one person shares his gifts in worship, he encourages another to share his gifts.

Teaching/learning has a great deal in common with worship. In fact, it may be more appropriate to call worship "worship/service." True worship results in service; teaching results in learning. Biblically, to learn is to serve. We teach so that others may learn; we worship so that we might serve better. To serve God better, we must learn of the God we serve and the needs of His people. Genuine worship should inspire, guide, and nurture our Christian teaching/learning.

The Children's Sermon

"Isn't that cute," the young mother said. Her eyes beamed with admiration and devotion. "The minister's children's sermons are so inspirational."

"Yes, I know, I must get more out of them than the children," her own mother responded.

This conversation capsulizes the spirit of many children's sermons or children's messages. These messages have become commonplace among churches of various denominations. Those with the responsibility for conducting children's sermons are always looking for a book of ideas or "sermon outlines." A search exists for the best type of information to be shared with children. While this chapter will not provide outlines of children's sermons, it will provide an examination of children's sermons and ways of improving its message.

The children's sermon is often one of the most misunderstood and misused of religious education practices. While it is highly popular, it is nevertheless often used inappropriately. While this misuse is not done intentionally, it happens just the same. The problem is simple. We prepare and deliver the children's sermon with the eyes, the ears, and the mind of an adult—not a child.

What are the eyes, the ears, and the mind of an adult? The adult mind is capable of using symbols and making comparisons between objects and other situations. An adult is able to infer comparisons from the concrete to the abstract. What appears understandable and logical to an adult does not to a child. Adults prepare and evaluate as adults, not as children. When other adults listen to the children's sermon, they hear with the adult ears, not the child's ears. The major problem stated simply is—we do not consider our audience.

Common Mistakes in Children's Sermons

Inappropriate Language

One of the most wonderful gifts we possess is language. Language allows us to communicate truth, to establish relationships, and to nurture fellowship with others. By its very nature, language also allows us to communicate falsehoods, to destroy relationships, and to hinder fellowship with others.

The language we use must be appropriate to those with whom we are communicating. Examine the language used as you talk with a child. Adult language is filled with symbols, metaphors (comparisons), and figurative language. However, this is no problem, for we adults know exactly what we are communicating. In contrast, the child does not yet understand these figurative facets of human language. Using the language of adults with children leads to natural and expected misunderstandings.

While children understand language quite literally, adults use language figuratively. Our figurative language is taken for granted; we assume everyone understands our intents. However, children understand in ways different from that of an adult. We must not take our language for granted. We must choose our words deliberately. Otherwise, we may confuse children.

Improper Object Usage

Quite common in the children's sermon is the use of objects. These objects generally introduce the content of the message. In addition, these objects are concrete examples to introduce abstract ideas to children.

One problem is that the objects tend to become an end in themselves with the child. The child becomes fascinated and preoccupied with the object. Children fidgeting for the object have difficulty concentrating on the words of the speaker. Children are often unable to make the transition from the concrete object to an abstract principle. However, objects may be used. Select objects carefully so that they arouse initial interest. Then focus attention upon the heart of what is being conveyed.

Lengthy Presentations

Often the presentation of the message is too lengthy for the attention span of the listening children. While an adult may wish the message to continue, the children quickly become bored. The message must be brief and to the point. Otherwise a child will lose his concentration and focus attention elsewhere.

Wrong Audience

The audience or target group for the children's sermon is often not the children. Rather, it is the adult congregation. Care must be noted that the presentation is given to the children and not to the adults.

This trap catches many of us. We like the attention and praise of our peers. Adults often comment on how wonderful the children's sermons are. Well, the sermons may be wonderful; however, the general focus of attention is often the adult. The adult understands and appreciates the complexities of the message. Thus, it is natural for the conveyer to seek reinforcement from adults by providing messages that appeal to them. This trap involves our choosing the words and concepts that appeal to adults.

Inappropriate Motivation

What is the motivation behind the children's sermon? Are egos involved? Is there a pressure to have something for the children? Are we too motivated by seeking the praise of other adults? The basic motivation must involve a sincere desire to present some information or convey some feeling to the child. Without this basic intent, the results are somewhat less than satisfactory. A good relationship should exist between the children and the storytellers. We are there to help the children. Anything less is inappropriate.

Diverse Groups

Children's messages are often directed at an audience comprised of four to eight year olds. What a difference in ability and understanding! Examine the children who come forward during the children's time. What is their age range? Is there a large range between the children? Large age groups make effective communication more difficult. If diverse age groups exist, alternative activities may be provided.

Guidelines for Planning the Children's Sermon

While the above discussion has centered upon mistakes made in children's sermons, the children's sermon has merit if properly planned and delivered. The following guidelines are offered.

1. Keep the cognitive development of the child in mind as you prepare the children's sermon.

The child between the ages of two to seven. The child's thinking is primarily egocentric. He only knows his own viewpoint. The child is unable to understand symbols; everything is taken literally. The child gives life-like qualities to inanimate objects. Everything happens for a special purpose; this purpose centers around the child and his experience.

The child between seven and eleven. During this age, the child is beginning to take the viewpoint of others. He can begin to take several situations into account in the solving of problems. His short-term and long-term memory has greatly improved. The child is beginning to think logically, but must have concrete examples in his thinking. There is more than one answer to a situation. His language skills are improving.

2. Summarize the major idea or theme that you wish to convey to the children. What basic message do you wish to convey? What do you wish the child to carry away from the experience? Keep the message simple and something easily applicable to the child's mind. For the younger child, ideas around such themes as Jesus, God, family, church, home, friends, nature, and our world may prove to be helpful. What ideas or feelings about these themes should be conveyed to the child? Be specific. Stick to one idea for each message.

3. Select carefully any learning aids that will assist you in demonstrating the lesson. Let the lesson choose the learning aid. Do not allow the learning aid to select the lesson. The learning aids, especially objects, should be used to focus attention to the main message.

4. Practice your presentation. Keep in mind the words that you use. Are these words appropriate to the children who are listening? Parents and other adults should not be your primary consideration in dealing with children's sermons. Watch your time element. Their attention span is limited; generally focus around three to five minutes.

5. Focus on your relationship with the children beyond the children's sermon. We teach primarily through relationships. Focus upon building a relationship that will enhance the teaching/learning process. Showing love and kindness is important before and after the worship service, as well as during the children's sermon.

6. Involve the children in other aspects of the worship service. Do not allow the children's sermon to be the only way for the child to be involved. Work with parents and other staff members to find ways of

meaningfully involving the children in worship. Provide guidelines or suggestions for parents to use while the child is sitting on the pew. Use hymns that appeal to children. Let the children participate in ways that are appropriate. Children are a part of the church. Involve them appropriately and lovingly.

Reviewing the Opportunity

The worship service offers unique opportunities for teaching/learning experiences for the congregation. In no other location do we have so many participants. To improve the teaching/learning goal, we must first analyze the worship service. Next careful planning should be done to improve the educational experience for all age participants. In particular, children's sermons, if used, should be done at a level appropriate for the children. Careful analysis and planning will improve what we remember and what we do as a result of having worshiped.

Notes

1. Philip Wendell Crannell, "Worship," *International Standard Bible Encyclopedia,* Eerdsman, 1957, p. 3110.

The following books may be helpful in teaching/learning through the worship service.

Bailey, Robert, *New Ways In Christian Worship.* Broadman, 1981.

Breeden, Ed., *Worship Services For Special Occasions.* Baker House, 1989.

Linam, Gail, *The Bible Speaks To Children.* Broadman, 1989.

———— *God's People: A Book of Children's Sermons.* Broadman, 1986.

Martin, Thielman, *Getting Ready For Sunday: A Practical Guide for Worship Planning.* Broadman, 1989.

Segler, Franklin M. *Christian Worship: Its Theology and Practice.* Broadman, 1975.

Webber, Robert E. *Worship Is A Verb.* Word, 1987.

Wright, Una. *For Children Only: Sermons For Younger Children.* Broadman, 1989.

9. Leadership Training

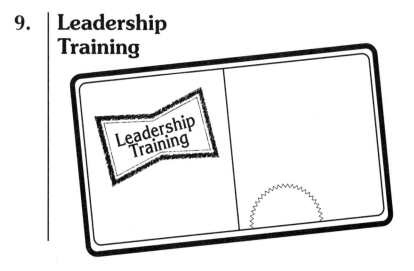

Establishing Importance

"Leaders are born. You certainly cannot make a leader," the younger churchman stated.

"I disagree. Leaders can be made through proper training," retorted the older churchman.

These two positions reflect two opposing views on leadership. In the first view, leadership is an inborn characteristic and cannot be acquired or taught. The second view involves leadership as an art to be learned, like any other skill. The best or most accurate position may recognize the merit in both positions. Unquestionably, a leader's success may have certain characteristics such as honesty, fairness, thoroughness and good social skills. However, certain characteristics may be acquired through practice. This chapter will focus on those ways in which leadership training can be used to enhance the teaching/learning of the church.

Imagine yourself with the opportunity to be trained by any individual in the history of the world. What would you wish to be trained to do? Who would be your teacher? If you were a nurse, you might choose Clara Barton or Florence Nightingale. If you were a golfer, would you choose Jack Nicklaus? If you were a business person, would you choose to be instructed by Lee Iococoa? If you are a church leader, who would you chose to be your teacher?

Regardless of our present skill level, we benefit from leadership training opportunities. Businesses and professional groups recognize this fact. Many professional organizations require their membership to engage in a specific number of continuing education credits during a given time period. Teachers, accountants, health care professionals, counselors, and business leaders must constantly engage in continuing education. If this need is essential in the secular/professional world, what about the Christian world?

Leadership training offers tremendous potential for both the life of individuals and the life of the church. Individuals may identify new gifts or areas of service; skills may be sharpened for growth; and experiences may be shared that will instruct and inspire others.

Leadership training is broader in scope than the on-going Bible teaching program or Sunday School. However, the basic task is the same. Leadership Training seeks to identify, strengthen, and equip individuals with leadership skills and qualities. These qualities should enhance the proclamation of the gospel. Both the individual and the church benefit.

Like the wide variety of persons and needs, various types of leadership training are available. These programs prepare persons for leadership roles in church programs and educational organizations such as Sunday School, deacon ministry, committee work, and mission organizations. Leadership training may involve ongoing studies such as survey courses in Old and New Testament, church history, missions, and theology. Discipleship may be the focus of leadership training including prayer, Bible study, and witnessing. It involves learning how to be a better parent, a better worker, a better citizen—a better proclaimer of the gospel. A broad concept, leadership training develops skills, attitudes, and knowledge for living the Christian life.

Leadership training is a special time of interaction between learner and teacher. As He worked with His twelve disciples, Jesus engaged in intensive leadership training. These disciples would assume leadership positions that would alter the course of world history. In these intensive teaching/learning experiences, new growth can occur.

Defining Chapter Goals

At the conclusion of this chapter, the learner should be able to do the following:
- identify and describe basic guidelines for leadership training;
- draw and explain a basic model for leadership training;
- identify and discuss twelve guidelines in planning a retreat or conference; and
- identify resources for planning training opportunities.

Guidelines for Adult Training

Survey

To survey means to explore and to determine what needs currently exist. In leadership training, we must survey three basic areas: the church, the world, and the individual. Each of these areas can provide information for developing needed leadership.

The church.—Take a long and thoughtful look at your local church. What areas of your church need specialized leadership skills? Are there areas of ministry that are neglected? What are the potential areas of growth? Identifying needed leadership skills is the first step in developing a leadership training program. Begin with the church as you identify areas of need. Consult the church's key leadership to determine areas of need. Information gathered can be the core for future plans and programming.

The world.—On first glance, the world may first appear a strange place to consult in determining topics for Christian leadership training. However, if Christians are to be a key force in the world, they need training. Examining the newspaper can often provide information concerning where leadership training is needed. For example, social problems are easily recognized as potential growth areas. Christians need to discover their role in meeting hunger, in helping the homeless, in fighting pornography, and in preventing child abuse. Discovering your role involves not only recognizing a need but also developing concrete helping skills. Filling in the blank, "what my world (my community) needs now is _____," may provide key information for the content of leadership training.

The individual.—Although often ignored in the educational process, the individual often knows his own needs for growth and development. Surveying the members of the congregation may determine areas where growth training is needed. Varied needs and interest will appear. Offer what people express as interests and needs. Let them be involved in the planning of their own educational growth. We participate in what we believe in!

Identify Leadership

After needs have been identified, identify potential leadership. Look for leadership in many places, in the obvious and not so obvious. Often if the church is near a university or seminary or has a number of seminary-trained members, this group becomes the only group from which trainers/teachers are selected. If this pattern continues, the church may develop the mistaken belief that if leadership training is to occur, it must develop from this elite group. If the church develops such an attitude, it misses other potential and capable leaders. Great strides in the church occur when laypeople are involved. Laypeople are the church.

Broaden the concept of leadership. Many church members have specialized skills that can be shared in the context of Christian leadership. These include teachers, lawyers, secretaries, businessmen, nurses, doctors, or farmers. These individuals may or may not be seminary-trained; however, they may have abilities that can enrich the lives of others through various teaching/learning experiences. Farmers and housewives may share ways to supplement food in difficult economic times. Teachers can help in teaching core skills for those working in literacy missions. Businessmen may help young families to manage their financial resources. Lawyers can instruct in how to be a good steward of our resources, both now and later. By virtue of their Christian discipleship, many individuals are especially equipped to help others in their Christian life and service. Whatever gifts you possess can be used to further the mission of the church.

Leadership Training Program

Usage and practice are key elements in our understanding of words, ideas, and concepts. A chalkboard does not function as a chalkboard until we use it. We do not understand the capabilities of word processing until we practice it ourselves. Being a singer does not become a reality until we first sing. True understanding is enhanced by practice.

Similarly, leadership training is no training until it is practiced. Through instructing His disciples, Jesus provided opportunities for developing their newly acquired knowledge, skill, and attitudes. Sometimes Jesus' followers succeeded; sometimes they failed. However, they were trained by being given opportunities. Leadership training must be characterized by active participation and application.

A simplified formula for leadership training of any type is *Input*, *Practice*, *Response*, and *Feedback*. This simple formula provides guidelines for teaching/learning. *Input* involves the sharing of information, the demonstration of a skill or the sharing of an attitude. Input provides information to the learner. The input may come from a teacher, a video presentation, a book, or numerous other forms. Nevertheless, input is the direct instruction given. Training involves some type of input. For example, if you're training someone to conduct a business meeting, input may be a lecture from a teacher, a video presentation of an actual meeting or reading a book on parliamentarian procedures. Without some type of input, how would we know what we are trying to develop?

Practice involves activities in which the learner has opportunities to use the newly acquired "input." Practice should actively use the learner's various senses. The more sense involvement, the greater the likelihood of improving learning. Break conducting a meeting into its various elements, such as calling the meeting together, recognizing a speaker, making a motion, and voting on a motion. Have the learner practice these various elements in different ways, such as explaining the procedure, answering questions about the information, or demonstrating the various skills. Practice may not always make perfect; however, practice does contribute to improvement.

Response involves an opportunity, apart from practice, in which the learner can demonstrate his mastery of the material, the skill, or the attitude. The type of response offered varies with the type of information under study. Providing real-to-life opportunities to demonstrate the material makes for a better test or examination of response. If you're training someone to conduct a business meeting, let him conduct a meeting in a live setting. It's a great way to learn.

Feedback, the exchange of information on performance, is crucial in leadership training. Individuals need to know how well they are doing in the teaching/learning process. Feedback may help to correct any false ideas and any inadequate parts of a skill being demonstrated. Occurring throughout the process, feedback provides ways of improvement.

A Model of Leadership Training

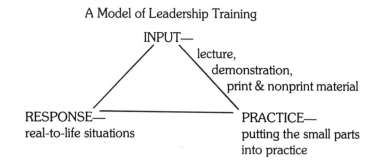

INPUT—
lecture,
demonstration,
print & nonprint material

RESPONSE—
real-to-life situations

PRACTICE—
putting the small parts
into practice

Unlike a traditional report card that may damage the individual's self-concept, feedback in Christian teaching/learning should focus upon ways of improvement. If we receive feedback early, we may be able to avoid future problems. In the above example, give learners feedback about their performance in conducting the business session. Feedback should lead toward improvement.

Retreats or Conferences

One special avenue for leadership training involves the retreat or the special conference. Participants find that retreats offer distinct advantages for teaching/learning interactions. In a special atmosphere, interruptions are minimal. Away from the hectic demands of daily life, the time can be both motivational and inspirational. New relationships can begin; old relationships can be both healed and strengthened. Retreats provide a special time of focusing upon your relationship with God.

Retreats or conferences can be conducted for any number of specialized leadership needs. Retreats may be focused upon various age groups, educational organizations, committees, family relations, Bible and doctrinal study, specialized ministries, holidays, and other specialized interests. While each retreat or conference is unique because of its specialized purpose, several guidelines are universal.

1. *Establish theme and goals.* Leaders and learners should work jointly in establishing the theme and goals of the retreat. What is the purpose of the retreat or conference? Be as specific as possible in the planning. Establish a broad general goal and subgoals which will aid in the accomplishment of the major or overarching goal. For example, the theme or goal may be "Strengthening Your Relationship with God." Subgoals may include a focus upon prayer, Bible study, and fellowship

with other Christians. These subgoals can be developed throughout the retreat with special sessions devoted to each one.

2. *Establish the target audience.* What age group or interest group is the conference directed toward? Will the target audience and the established theme and goals be compatible? Don't have a retreat for youth or college students that does not deal with relevant needs. What special needs or characteristics of the target audience must be considered when planning the retreat/conference? Are facilities available for the handicapped? Are there suitable areas for young children? Are there facilities and interests that will appeal to the target audience—children, youth, or adults?

3. *Establish the location.* What location is going to be the best for the conference? At the church building? Away from the church building? These considerations must be based upon anticipated attendance, available facilities, and financial considerations. While going away may be the ideal, it is still possible to have a good retreat/conference at the local church. Attitudes and expectations are crucial in the success of a retreat. Location does influence our attitudes and expectations.

4. *Establish the time.* Examine the church calendar to determine the best time for having the meeting. In addition, check the local school and community calendars. Relate the retreat's theme to the most appropriate time of year. For example, a retreat on financial planning would be excellent in the late fall as people prepare for a new year. As families contemplate family time in the summer, a spring retreat on family relations would be superb.

Try to avoid as many conflicts as possible. Keep in mind that avoiding all conflicts is impossible. Time conflict is a part of any activity. However, try to keep it minimal.

5. *Determine leadership needed.* Who will be needed for the various sessions in your retreat/conference? Enlist and train the workers early. Provide them with whatever materials are needed. Use a variety of people, those with proven talent and those with talent still-in-training.

6. *Schedule events.* Be realistic in what you wish to accomplish during the retreat/conference. While you want to have a quality program, do not defeat your own purpose by "overworking" your participants. After "input" sessions, schedule a change of pace. The mind can only absorb what the "seat" will allow. As a missionary journeyman (two-year volunteer in foreign missions), I underwent a six-week training session. Toward the end of the six weeks, I longed for our daily

recreation periods. By nature and practice, I am not athletically inclined. However, the recreation was a break that I looked forward to each day after hours of grueling "input."

Plan for periods of activity, as well as some periods of rest. Adequate rest, recreation, and food will greatly enhance the quality of the retreat/ conference. Ask how people will respond to the retreat's scheduled activities. Modify the schedule if needed.

7. *Plan for food.* Man may not live by bread alone; however, bread and peanut butter do help. Consider what types of food are appropriate for the meeting. Time spent at the retreat, availability of food, and time involved in preparation will determine the type of food and refreshments necessary. Will everyone be responsible for part of the preparation of refreshments? Will an outside group be responsible? Remember, the preparation of the food can be a time of fellowship building. Divide the group into teams for preparing the meals. Recognize the hard work of people. Make the entire food process—preparing, eating, and cleaning up—enjoyable.

8. *Plan for publicity.* Regardless of the amount of time spent in planning, the retreat/conference will have minimal impact if there is not good publicity. Assign one individual or a small committee to oversee the publicity. Include posters throughout the church, mailouts to potential retreat participants, articles in the church newsletter, and announcements from the pulpit and Sunday School departments. Good publicity will enhance the effectiveness of the retreat. Let people know what is happening.

9. *Work at communication.* Good communication is vital throughout the planning process. Conference leaders, participants, and other individuals need to be kept informed. It is best if the communication can be done in writing. A written memo can minimize misunderstandings. Communicate, and again I say communicate.

10. *Plan a detailed calendar and assignment sheet.* Use a calendar and assignment sheet to keep track of the progress of the retreat/ conference. Make job assignments. Check on individuals to determine how well the details are being conducted. The retreat leaders need to know how the planning and implementing phases are being conducted. Keep good records; don't rely on memory alone.

11. *Remember to evaluate.* The conference or retreat is not over until it has been evaluated. Include both leadership and participants in the evaluation. Evaluation can be used to improve future conferences

and retreats. Approach the evaluation as a positive experience, rather than a negative one. Let's evaluate so we can make it even better the next time.

12. *Give praise.* Use praise liberally throughout the retreat with both participants and leadership. Let people know that their participation makes a difference. Write thank you notes to your leadership. Do a write up in the church paper or newsletter. Share the success and events of the retreat through Sunday School classes and in the worship services. Encourage others to join you next time. In a friendly way, let people know what they missed by not attending. Encourage them now to plan to attend the next one.

Retreats can be a special time of intensive growth and development. Lives can be changed because of retreats. Although retreats are wonderful growth opportunities, they are costly. Time, energy, and planning are essential in a good retreat. If the retreat is worth doing, it is worth doing well.

Reviewing the Opportunity

Leadership Training events, such as retreats, conferences, special studies, or seminars, provide intensive training in the various aspects of Christian growth and ministry. Carefully planned opportunities have the potential for changing people's lives. Care must be used in selecting the material to be studied and in ways of presenting the material. Good teaching must occur both in the content and the context of the experience. Such intensive opportunities should be seriously explored by Christians as ways to improve their life and ministry.

Notes

The following books may help in teaching/learning through leadership training events and retreats:

Burt, Steve. *Activating Leadership in the Small Church.* Judson, 1988.

Chartier, Jan. *Developing Leadership in the Teaching Church.* Judson, 1985.

Clark, Chap. *Great Camps & Retreats.* Zondervan, 1990.

Edgemon, Roy T. *Discipleall: A Discipleship Training Manual.* Convention Press, 1990.

Elliott, Nilon, "101 Retreats." *Church Recreation Magazine,* XIV (July/August/September 1984) p. 48-50.

Inman, V. Kerry. *How To Make It Happen: Planning Church Events With Ease.* Zondervan, 1988.

Lee, Harris W. *Effective Church Leadership: A Practical Sourcebook.* Augsburg Fortress, 1989.

Messner, Robert C. *Leadership Development Through S.E.R.V.I.C.E.: An Ongoing Program for Equipping Servant Leaders in the Church.* Standard, 1988.

Reimer, Sandy & Reimer, Larry. *The Retreat Handbook.* Morehouse Publishing Company, 1987.

Shawchuck, Norman Job, Rueben P. & Doherty, Robert G. *How to Conduct A Spiritual Life Retreat.* The Upper Room Abingdon, 1986.

Smith, Frank Hart. *A Guide to Planning and Conducting A Retreat.* Convention Press, 1977.

10. Missions Education

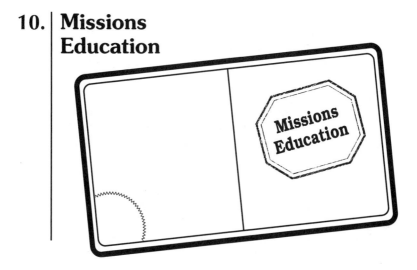

Establishing Importance

"Missions education" in the twentieth century? Missions is nineteenth century images with natives huddled in grass huts; missionaries with tropical hats; the famous missionary barrels filled with cast-off clothes and used tea bags; and teaching the basics of reading, writing, and arithmetic. Not in the twentieth century! We live in an age with super sonic jets and computer and communication systems that link the world as one community. Why should we have missions education?

To grasp the importance of missions education, it is essential to look to the Christian basis for missions—the Bible. The Word of God speaks directly to the issue of missions. Genesis describes the creation of the world and the creation of human beings. Mankind, given a special place in the created order, is to subdue and to have dominion over the world (Gen. 1:28). This instruction is not a command to engage in a mere population explosion. Rather, human beings are to disperse throughout the earth and to fill the earth with their influence. This idea, as developed later, has definite implications for missions education.

The famous call of Abram from the land of Ur to go to the land of Canaan has a missionary origin (Gen. 12). In spite of Abram's own failures, God made a covenant with Abram that through him many nations were to be blessed. Again these descendants of Abram (later called Abraham) are led by Moses from captivity to freedom. At Mount Sinai, God and His Chosen People entered into a covenant. If these people were faithful to Him, God would make of them a kingdom of priests—a holy nation.

The idea of a kingdom of priests and a holy nation is extremely important in missions. Those faithful to God are to be His priests. Being a priest involves serving both God and mankind. A holy nation is one having been separated for the purposes of God, including teaching others how to be holy. Those who are set apart for the exclusive purposes of God are indeed a part of the mission enterprise.

The New Testament provides a clear mandate (a royal command) for all disciples to be engaged in missions (Matt. 28:16-20). The Book of Acts gives evidence of these disciples (learners) carrying out this command of the Lord Jesus Christ. Paul is a vivid example of one who shared the Word to both the Jewish and Gentile world. The common theme, both in the Old Testament and New Testament, is to go forth and to give a witness that will influence the world for the purposes of God.

Before leaving the biblical mandate, it is crucial to emphasize that discipling is very much a part of the mission process. Abraham and Moses were taught by God through various learning experiences. As they responded to their lessons in faith, their particular mission in life was enlarged. Each experience brought them closer to God who called them. As evidenced in Scripture, Jesus spent a great deal of time in the discipleship process with His followers. Discipling involves following after the Master. Following Him involves going. Only those involved in discipleship will be equipped to teach and to observe all that Jesus has commanded. Both "disciple-ing" and missions travel in the same stream of life.

Defining Chapter Goals

Now that the learner is convinced of the importance of missions education, the learner shall now explore its teaching context. At the conclusion of this chapter, the learner should be able to do the following:

- describe the importance of missions education to the work and heritage of the church;
- identify and discuss the key educational components in missions education;

- state a formula for developing missions education goals;
- identify church life-style characteristics that promote missions and mission awareness;
- identify eleven guidelines for strengthening mission education programming;
- list alternatives to traditional mission study opportunities; and
- identify resources in missions education.

Educative Process

A church's and an individual's educational philosophy and theology of missions will determine the direction pursued in missions education. Such education must be experience oriented because of the very nature of missions. The biblical materials testify to the importance of experience in the life of God's people. Progressive education involves beginning at one known point and moving toward unknown points. From our known world we share the gospel with an unknown world. Missions education must be both experience-oriented and progressive. This understanding is part of the cutting edge of life itself.

The Learner

At the center of the education process is the learner. Faithful to the Hebrew model, the learner must be considered as a whole in the missions education endeavor. Individual differences must be considered. Basic to the Christian idea is the belief that God cares for all people. In missions education, the whole learner, with all strengths, weakness, successes, and failures, is vital. The goal of education is aiding the learner to develop the powers of reasoning—the ability to make intelligent choices. Missions education should aim toward developing individuals who can respond with greater accuracy and commitment to God's will for their individual lives.

The Teacher

The teacher in missions education should be a project director, learning leader, and a co-learner. In true missions education, the teacher should be learning more and more of God's grace and will for his own life. The teacher should be thoroughly prepared for both the spirit and the information that he seeks to communicate. This preparation includes a spiritual preparation.

The teacher must be a creative person who can encourage creativity in others. The teacher constructs learning activities that lead to mission education goals. In missions education, the teacher should be one who creatively shares his own experiences and who leads learners into new life experiences.

The Content

The content of missions education develops from the interaction of the gospel and the life concerns of the learner and the world. The gospel becomes alive when the learner experiences the reality of the gospel in his own life and concerns. The description of the curriculum should involve those points between the person and the gospel.

Traditionally, mission study has included the biblical message of missions, the contemporary missions scene, the history of missions, and spiritual growth. However, the subject of a total missions education program should not be limited to those materials that fit neatly into those categories. Rather, the curriculum of missions education should develop from the biblical message, the world situation (past, present, and future), and the learner/disciple.

Goals and Evaluation

Missions education should be based upon specific goals and evaluation techniques. We must decide what we want to accomplish whether it is the study of the life of a particular missionary, collecting food for the hungry, or adopting a missions offering goal. These goals should be developed by the church for the entire church and for each age group within the church. Mission education goals should flow directly from the church's goals or intents. In this respect, the missions education program is unified with the mission and goals of the church.

Without goals how can we evaluate? How will we know when we have met our goal unless it is stated? Evaluation techniques aid in determining the degree to which the goal has been reached. The following formula may be used in developing mission education goals:

Biblical Message, World Situation, and Learner Characteristics

MISSIONS EDUCATION GOALS

We evaluate ourselves in light of our goals. Our goals should be ones that will bring honor to God. Everything we do says something about our views and commitments to missions. The quality of our goals says something about the value we give life itself.

Missionary Heritage

As Christians, we are the heirs and the products of the missionary activities of past generations. All that we enjoy today is from the efforts of Christians of the past. Previous generations have established the foundations upon which we now live. Advances in the world have been brought about through the efforts of Christians. Included are advances in human rights and equality, health care, and education. Sadly, Christians have not always been the "light" and the "salt" of the earth.

Historically, missions has always been a part of the Christian church. The Christian movement began its missionary enterprise as believers traveled to various parts of the world, either by choice or through persecution. The church spread throughout the world. The church has been strongest during its times of greatest missionary activity. Initially, Christian believers were persecuted by government, such as the Roman Empire. In time, some governments became more receptive to the Christian faith. With Emperor Constantine in 324 B.C., Christianity became the official religion of the Roman Empire—the heritage of Western Civilization. The faith once persecuted had become the privileged faith.

During the sixteenth and seventeenth centuries, the renewal of the church and European colonial exploration of the New World heightened missionary zeal. Missionary endeavors were often dominated by the Roman Catholic Church, especially through the efforts of the Jesuits. Evangelical revivals of the eighteenth and nineteenth centuries combined with European imperialism opened new areas for Christian witness. Protestants in Europe formed various volunteer mission societies such as the Baptist Missionary Society (1792), the London Missionary Society (1795), the Netherlands Mission Society (1797), and the Basel Mission (1815). William Carey, missionary to India, is considered the founder of the modern missionary movement. The church of the emerging modern world recommitted itself to worldwide missions.

Today, the heritage of the church is involvement in missions. We are a product of the missionary vision of those who went before us; we are the providers of a mission vision for our present and future generations. World-wide changes are sweeping across the earth as these pages are written. Communist governments are changing. The Berlin Wall has fallen. Formerly totalitarian governments are becoming more democratic. Opportunities exist for Christian missionary activity that were not imagined several years ago. Our heritage, as well as our current world situation, demands the church to be engaged in missions education. Missions education prepares people to go and to share the gospel.

Church Life-style

Because missions education occurs within the context of the church, it is important to give a description of a life-style that promotes missions and mission awareness. In fact, the very life-style of the church is an indication of its missionary climate, motivation, or inclination. Characteristics of a church life-style promoting missions may include the following:

1. *Discipling.* The church must give priority to developing disciples who can assume their rightful place of spiritual leadership. Education, on both an individual and a group level, must occur. Those truly discipled in the faith are more naturally inclined and supernaturally empowered to share that faith.

Teaching and discipling opportunities must exist for all members of the family of God. Both sexes and all ages must be provided with an opportunity to learn and to do God's will. Discipleship opportunities must be offered as individuals mature in their understanding, attitudes, and abilities.

2. *Personal and active involvement.* Churches that share their gifts and talents are mission-oriented. Individuals should be privileged to discover their giftedness and how to use that giftedness in Christian service. The norm should be that members engage in Christian service and not the exception. Churches that share their gifts are mission-oriented.

3. *Church staff leadership.* The staff of the local church should be firmly committed to the missionary enterprise. Should the staff not be fervently committed to the cause of missions, less than effective missions education will occur. When staff are enthusiastically committed to missions, including missions education, their influence permeates the entire church.

4. *Bible-centered preaching and teaching.* The preaching and any other teaching opportunity must involve the Bible. The missionary imperative of the Bible must sound clearly and distinctly. Teaching the Bible will ultimately result in people engaged in mission activity. "Go" is the first two letters in the word *gospel.*

5. *No respecter of persons.* The missionary church is one that wel-

comes all into the kingdom. Such churches make efforts in their witness to cross racial, cultural, social, and economic barriers. A willingness to accept and to welcome all must exist.

6. *Atmosphere of expectation and energy.* The world changes when we expect it to do so and when we are willing to work. Our expectations influence our receptivity to God's working in our lives. The missionary church is one that has energy and expectation. Every part of church life should be permeated with the expectation and commitment to do God's work. We become motivated for Christian life and service.

7. *Mission support.* Specific time, talent, and finances must be devoted to the support of missions. This support involves prayer support, ranging from specific prayer groups to praying for missions in the worship service. Examine the church budget and the church calendar. Much can be learned about the commitment to missions.

8. *Goals and evaluation.* Goals can lead us toward growth; evaluation helps us know how we are growing. The setting of goals indicates a measure of commitment to something. Churches with specific goals and methods of measuring the achievement of those goals are more apt to plan for growth. Planning for growth and development is an important ingredient in mission promotion.

9. *Healthy fellowship.* Churches are involved in relationships ranging from the large group worship to the small group involvement. Some fellowships promote good health; others promote poor health. Healthy fellowships provide good relationships for those within the group and for those outside the group.

We must reach out to others to bring them into the family. Once in the family, they must be sustained through nurturing relationships. Either extreme leads to destruction. In the former instance, we may bring large numbers in only to lose them. In the later instance, we keep what we currently have without regard to further growth. Churches with a healthy balance of working within and working without have the vision for missions involvement.

Strengthening Missions Education Programming

The following guidelines will enhance the mission teaching/learning opportunities within the church:

1. *Give priority to Scripture.* In any mission program, relate the study to Scripture. Let the credibility of Scripture contribute to your own program. Without a genuine Scriptural base, missions loses its powers.

To the listener, Scripture has priority. Use that priority as you lead in mission awareness.

2. *Involve both men and woman as participants.* Missions education activities have the stereotype of being only for the "little, old ladies." Enlist some key men who can model the way for other men to participate. By the same token, enlist young professional women to model ways for other women to participate. If a missions education program is effective, it must involve all members of the congregation— young and old, men and women.

3. *Provide a variety of leaders.* The greater the variety of individuals leading the study, the better. Have both men and women participate. Involve the youth and children. Internationals, often found in your community, can provide insight into life and the Christian faith of their culture. Don't neglect other individuals who are not paid religious workers. Businessmen, servicemen, and diplomatic corps workers can provide new information and insight for people.

4. *Make the missionary real.* Missionaries are saints, aren't they? Yes and no. We have a tendency to make the missionary an idol or icon. Missionaries are godly people, but people nevertheless. Show them the real struggles, fears, frustrations, as well as accomplishments, joys, and victories of being a missionary. Invite furloughing missionaries not only to speak in formal settings, but also to participate in class fellowships and church socials. By making the missionary real, you may encourage others to listen and to respond to God's leadership.

5. *Relate the program to the developmental needs of the hearers.* Use whatever bridges or common interests possible to make the transition from the study to everyday concerns. If the group is comprised of older men, speak about the life of similar men in the overseas setting and give examples of how men of this age can serve. Talk about the games children play if children are in your audience. Describe the joys and frustrations and humor of overseas mothers if your group is comprised of mothers. Let programs speak to persons.

6. *Be well-prepared in any presentation.* Don't read a program. Such ill-prepared programs do not reinforce the credibility of the mission education program. Pastors are less likely to give pulpit time to poorly planned mission programs. Being thorough will increase the likelihood of additional program opportunities. Prepare and practice.

7. *Provide special activities that involve the various senses of the participants.* Have activities that will appeal to the sight, sound, taste,

and touch of individuals. Bring food and artifacts from other countries. Dress up in national attire and use music from an overseas country. Make the experience real, as if the person were actually there.

8. *Provide and suggest challenging activities.* Don't just present information. With each presentation have some type of challenge. If its just information, what difference has it made? Give the listeners something they can personally do, such as write a letter to a new Christian, pray for a specific item, collect certain items for a project, or volunteer time in a day-care center. Challenge them to do something in light of the program presented.

9. *Provide opportunity for feedback of new activities, mission projects, and goals.* Let people report on what they are doing or have been inspired to do. Send people out; but bring them back for periodic reports. Let feedback be a way of providing new information and new opportunity.

10. *Relate one study to other previous studies.* Help individuals to discover the connection between what is studied yesterday, what is studied today, and what will be studied tomorrow. Demonstrate the unity to the "wonderful madness and activity" of missions.

11. *Relate the missions programming to other major groups within the church.* Let missions be a part of the entire church's life-style. Seek cooperation and support from other groups; be cooperative and supportive of other program groups. Help the church to work together in promoting the kingdom of God—a lifelong mission project.

One Hundred Alternatives to
Traditional Mission Study Opportunities

Missions education is as broad and varied as the needs and interests of people. Use variety and challenge in presenting missions information. The following suggestions may inspire you to innovate and to create vital mission study and mission action opportunities. Only brief titles are given. Use your imagination to fill in the rest.

1. Service Opportunity Presentations
2. Mission Tours
3. Bulletin Boards
4. Mission Action Projects
5. Mission Resource Shops
6. Missions Fairs
7. Calendar of Prayer
8. Adopt a Missionary
9. Missionary Guest
10. Missionary Testimonies
11. Mission Dramas

12. Mission Musicals
13. Mission Hotlines
14. Mission Dinner-on-the-Grounds
15. Missionary Moments in Pre-offertory Periods
16. Lay Testimonies of Missionary Involvements
17. Bulletin and Periodical Inserts
18. Departmental Emphases
19. Multi-Media Presentations
20. Choral Readings
21. Pantomimes
22. World Mission Conferences
23. Pictures
24. Art From Around the World
25. Missions Night in Special Study Sessions
26. Tour of Mission Sending Agencies
27. Communications with Missionaries on the Field
28. Missionary Kid Testimonies
29. Singing
30. Stewardship Emphases
31. Missionary Birthday Parties
32. Films
33. Tape Recordings
34. Missionary Reading Clubs for Children
35. Scripture Memorization
36. Missionaries as Preachers
37. Adopt a Foreign Mission
38. Mission Fashion Show
39. Mission Olympics
40. Mission Puppets
41. Local Newspaper Promotions

42. Special Mission Conference Centers
43. Slide-Prayer Presentations
44. Mission Bake Off
45. Stamp Collection
46. Coins of the World
47. Mission Assimilation Games
48. Role Playing
49. Mission Monologues
50. Printed T-Shirts
51. Mission Prayer Partners
52. Sermon Interpretation in Various Languages
53. Jogging for Missions
54. Billboards
55. Missions Lock-In
56. Hobbies around the World
57. Children's Games Around the World
58. Vacations at Mission Points
59. Missionary Maps on Display
60. New-Member Orientation Pack Containing Mission Materials
61. Mission Jigsaw Puzzles
62. Mission Magazine of the Local Church
63. Missionary Residences
64. Missions Tea
65. Missions Open House
66. Missions Scavenger Hunts
67. Mission Support Variety Show
68. Mission Murals
69. Hymns Around the World
70. Telephone Missionaries During Worship Services
71. Mission Personnel Testimonies

72. Family Mite (Savings) Box
73. Family Worship
74. Adopt a Church in a Pioneer Area
75. You Are There Presentations
76. Mission Scholarships
77. Week-day Ministries
78. Summer Missions Deputation Teams
79. On-the-Job Training
80. Multi-Media Presentation of Mission Funding Program
81. Post Office at Christmas Time
82. Special Local Church Mission Commissioning Services
83. Appropriate Awards for Mission Achievement
84. Staff Swap with a Mission Setting for a Given Time
85. Mission Education Helps in Denominational Papers
86. Mission Treasure Hunt
87. Retreats
88. Dinner Theatre
89. Exchange Students
90. Radio, Television Announcements
91. Church Subscriptions to Various Mission Magazines
92. Portraits of Christ Around the World
93. Easter Celebration Around the World
94. Christmas Traditions Around the World
95. Missionary Modes of Transportation
96. Historical Missionary Monologues
97. Childrens' Songs Around the World
98. Customs Across the Globe
99. Christian Books from Past to Present
100. "My Church" Mission Magazine

Reviewing the Opportunity

Missions education offers unique opportunities for individuals to engage in innovative Christian teaching/learning opportunities. Missions is a basic part of the Christian experience that must be shared by each new generation of Christians. Each generation must discover for itself how it can accomplish this God-given command. Building upon the lessons and strengths of past experiences, missions education can reach out to unexplored ways of teaching and preaching the Gospel. The harvest is truly plentiful for those willing to be a part of the harvesting.

Notes

The following books may be helpful in teaching/learning through missions education.

Peters, George. *A Biblical Theology of Missions.* Moody, 1972.

Robison, Jarene' Serratt, Mary Lou and Sutton, Jan. *Ideas For Exciting Mission Study.* Woman's Missionary Union, 1989.

Watson, Charlotte. *100 Plus Ways to Involve People in Missions.* Woman's Missionary Union, 1990.

Eerdman's *Handbook to the World's Religions.* Grand Rapids: Eerdman's Pub. Co., 1982.

Williamson, Nancy S. *52 Ways to Teach Missions.* San Diego: Rainbow, 1990.

Willis, T. Avery, Jr. *Biblical Basis of Missions.* Convention Press, 1985.

11. Mission Activities

Establishing Importance

This title may seem closely related to the previous one dealing with missions education. Although similar, the focus is a different one. Here we are addressing the issue of providing teaching/learning experiences for those outside of our established church structure. Often this venture will take various forms such as mission trips, vacation Bible schools, youth meetings, Backyard Bible Clubs, or other special emphases. Teaching in these situations requires additional preparation, skill, and patience.

We live in a world that is far from the ideal. Because of living in a sinful world, we have people who have special needs. In the teaching/learning process we must seek to address these special needs. Failure to do so will result in concern that is less than Christian. Numerous volumes could be written, and rightly so, on the special needs of learners. All groups of people (including the rich and socially advantaged) have special needs. However, the focus of this brief analysis will be upon the disadvantaged.

Historically, Christian teaching/learning has found a special opportunity of ministry among the disadvantaged of the world. Here the Word of God has provided hope, instruction, and light. Disadvantaged lives have been given the advantage of hearing and responding to the gospel message. Working with the disadvantaged offers special consideration. A few key ideas will now be shared on its importance.

Characteristics of the disadvantaged may include negative attitude toward school; vocational orientation rather than academic orientation; poor health and diet; disturbed family life; limited reading and language skills; poor school survival skills; preference for practical, rather than theoretical; slower rate of learning; and poor self-concept.[1]

The wise teacher must address these needs of the learner. Biehler summarizes some helpful suggestions for teaching the disadvantaged by meeting any existing deficiency needs such as physiological, safety, belonging, self-esteem; maximizing attractions and minimizing dangers of growth choices; developing realistic levels of success, expectation and self-esteem; avoiding excessive nonproductive competition; enhancing the desire to achieve; concentrating upon natural interests, creating new ones and encouraging learning for the sake of learning; and providing incentives and encouragement for learning.[2]

Defining Chapter Goals

At the conclusion of this chapter, the learner should be able to do the following:

- identify characteristics of disadvantaged learners and implications for teaching;
- discuss the importance of advanced preparation—spiritual, physical, and educational;
- identify guidelines for working with the disadvantaged in various settings;
- discuss the use of discipline in working with children; and
- identify resources for mission activities.

Preparing for the Teaching/Learning

Like other activities of the church, mission activities are dependent upon volunteer leadership. These leaders will make sacrifices in terms of time and energy to become a part of the process. The following guidelines are offered to help make their teaching/learning experience more profitable for both the volunteer teacher and for the learners.

Advance preparation is crucial. While this admonition applies to all teaching/learning situations, it is especially vital in mission type settings. In these settings, intensive daily teaching may occur in a week filled with numerous activities such as surveying the community, door-to-door witnessing, preaching in revival services, counseling the troubled, providing health care, and ministering to social needs. Time is at a premium.

Three areas of preparation include spiritual, physical, and educational. In terms of spiritual preparation, spend the time needed in prayer and Bible study, dedicating yourself to be God's instrument during this special time. The amount of time spent will make a great difference in the lives of those with whom you work and in your own life. Continue to spend the time in spiritual preparation each day of the activity. Regardless of the number of surprise events or mishaps, give thanks to God. An attitude of genuine thankfulness in your heart will be conveyed to those with whom you work.

Try to plan your preparation in advance so that you will be as rested as possible before the activities. Often we have a great deal of last minute preparation. How restful is it to get ready for a vacation? The family vacations I have known consist of days of preparation. By the time we arrive at the vacation site, we are tired and grumpy. People often joke about having to return to work to rest up after their vacation. Preparing early can make both the journey and the destination more enjoyable.

Being rested influences your attitude and your openness to the children and adults with whom you work. Try to have periods of rest during the time. Learn to say no even to a "fun activity" (staying up all night talking) when it may help in your own work (being prepared to teach in the morning). Try to eat nutritionally and on time. Take nutritious snacks along with you. Don't live on fast foods. Fast foods can be fun, but they can take away from your nutrition and productivity.

Be thoroughly familiar with the materials that you will teach. Rehearse the materials. Don't wait until the night or morning before to read the lesson for the first time. Prepare the learning activities in advance. The more preparation done beforehand, the more you will enjoy the teaching/learning opportunities. Try to keep your materials simple. You may not always be sure of what you will have—electricity, water, lighting. If water is needed for clean up or other projects, bring water along in a spray bottle. Try to keep the activities as simple and convenient as possible. Be innovative.

General Guidelines

The following guidelines may help in working with the disadvantaged in various types of mission settings.

1. *Use positive language.* Be careful that the language you use is positive and not condescending ("put down"). Avoid the use of such words as "poor," "low class," and "down and out." These words influence how others respond to you and to your message. Remember the golden rule: "Do unto others as you would have others do unto you." Use words that convey friendship and concern.

2. *Don't blame the victim.* We have a tendency in our culture to blame the victim of a misfortune. This blaming can vary from the birth of a mentally retarded child, to the occurrence of a sexual molestation, the loss of a job, and the disability from an illness to living in poverty. Objectively, we may argue that people are not responsible for these misfortunes. Subjectively, we may subtly believe they brought these misfortunes upon themselves.

One reason for blaming the victim is that it protects us. If we believe that misfortune can occur to any one, we are not comforted. If tragedy can befall anyone, then it can befall us. However, if tragedy comes to those who deserve it, then we can at least work toward not deserving it.

If we do blame the victim, it influences how we treat the individual. We may not have as much patience as we need. We may not use as much energy because we feel "what's the use; they aren't going to change anyway." Ideas we have about people shape our concern and our behavior toward them. Christians should be careful not to blame the victim. Scriptures teach that misfortunes and difficulty can occur to both the wise and the foolish (Matt. 7:24-27).

3. *Recognize other religious backgrounds.* Often those in mission activities have faith backgrounds different from our own. Some people may have no religious background. The things we take for granted may be foreign to them. As a summer missionary in New York, I extended an invitation at the close of the sermon. I expected everyone to know what an invitation was. Afterwards a friendly pastor explained to me that the people present did not know what was involved in the invitation. What I took for granted was a new experience for them. Next time I was more careful both in time and words to explain what would occur during the time of invitation.

It is important to recognize that other Christian traditions and practices are real and meaningful. Don't focus on making everyone Baptist, Methodist, Presbyterian, or whatever your own denomination is. Focus on presenting the gospel and encouraging Christian living. The matter of denominations should not be a primary concern or thrust. In missions, focus on presenting the gospel, not a denomination. If the person joins your denomination, fine. If they remain in their own denomination or choose to join another, fine. The most important goal is to help them to become a Christian. Then help them to find a place of worship appropriate for them.

4. *Don't belittle people.* It is important that we not say or do things that hurt people. We belittle people, however, if we talk about the dirtiness of a certain neighborhood. We may belittle if we talk about homes without fathers as being bad. We may belittle if we criticize those of other religious faiths. We may belittle people if we talk about certain behaviors or languages.

Care must be used as we seek to uplift, not to degrade people. If we set a pattern of belittling other people, the child or adult present will soon learn that we may belittle or degrade them. People who feel belittled are less likely to respond to our teaching/learning.

5. *Recognize cultural differences.* Cultural differences are indeed important. If we are to lead in teaching others, we must learn of their culture and respect it. For example, in interacting with some Orientals, it is important not to point the soul of your foot toward them or to touch someone on the head. These are cultural traditions that are taboo. To do so is to insult the people. Take time to learn of cultural differences and traditions important in the group. Talk with other ministers or missionaries for help and understanding. For people to hear our message, we must be respectful of them as persons.

6. *Use hand projects/crafts.* Today we have often gotten away from the use of projects and crafts. We are too sophisticated. However, projects and crafts have value, especially for those who are disadvantaged. A macaroni necklace, a picture made of dry beans, or hand puppets may not appeal to all. However, to some individuals, these little things are important. Sometimes a picture from Bible school will brighten a drab corner of someone's room.

Having material for children to bring home is a good reinforcer for them of what they have learned and experienced in the activity. If they have enjoyed making the project, they may come back the next day for more fun and activity. Taking the material home is a good reminder to parents of what their children are learning. Although the material may end up on the parking lot, it may end up in a home where it can be a positive witness for the gospel.

7. *Be prepared for potential discipline problems.* Discipline problems often arise regardless of the socio-economic level of children and youth. Being unruly is not just a problem with the disadvantaged. You can do

several things to minimize discipline problems from developing. First, let the group know the rules and how they will be enforced. Knowing from the beginning what is expected is important. Keep to those rules. If possible, allow the group to help in establishing the rules. Second, plan activities to keep the children and you busy. If you keep them busy, you are less likely to have discipline problems. Being bored leads to disruption. Also having to wait for the teacher to decide what to do next tempts children to misbehavior.

Third, if you must correct a child, make sure the punishment fits the crime. Don't punish on the first offense. Make sure the child or youth knows when the rules have been violated. When they know and continue to do so, choose something appropriate. Fourth, after discipline or correction has occurred, work at reestablishing the relationship. Bring the "offender" back into the group. Give them responsibility. The most important item we teach is relationships. Work at maintaining the relationships, even with disruptive people.

Misbehavior is often the result of seeking attention. Try to reinforce and give positive attention. Looking at the cause of the misbehavior can help in knowing what to do. Have a wide variety of techniques to draw upon when there is a need for a behavior change. Methods used over and over loose their effectiveness. Variety is the spice of discipline.

8. *Be prepared for the unexpected.* Don't be shocked at children who share horror stories about their home lives. Few children have ideal family situations. Be cautious, taking care of how much truth you give to what children say. Believe, but believe cautiously and maturely. Children may use bad language to shock you. Try not to be shocked. Often children will use language or convey information in an attempt to impress or to anger a teacher. Be prepared. Respond calmly.

9. *Remember missions can be an everyday activity.* Don't overlook the small opportunities to do mission work. Waiting for the organized vacation Bible school or the Bible club may cause you to miss important opportunities. Mission activities may be as simple as sharing flowers with a neighbor, offering a ride to an older person, listening to the excitement of a young child. Look for mission opportunities where you are. Significant moments can occur as you are waiting for a bus, eating in a restaurant, or buying groceries for a fellowship. Take the time to be open to God's leadership.

Remember the story of the good Samaritan (Luke 10:30-37). The priest and the Levite were too busy to become involved in the everyday mission opportunities that were literally at their feet. Being preoccupied to get to the temple may make us miss opportunities along the way. Be like the good Samaritan who noticed and responded to people along the way.

10. *Be prepared to be blessed.* Expect to be blessed by other people. You do not always bring the blessing to someone else, sometimes they bring it to you. Our faith can be strengthened by the most unlikely people. Be sensitive to the work of God in and through other people. Often blessings are missed because we fail to recognize and to receive them. Keep your sensitivity alive.

Reviewing the Opportunity

Christian teaching and learning opportunities must be extended to all individuals. Jesus told of a man who gave a great banquet and his honored guests failed to attend. The man then turned to invite others to participate in the feast (Matt. 22:1-10). As Christians we cannot limit ourselves to those who already know the gospel; we must open ourselves to all people. Learning how to teach the disadvantaged in various settings requires commitment. Regardless of socioeconomic class, each person is disadvantaged if he does not know Jesus Christ as Savior. We were all disadvantaged at one time. Those who are advantaged with Christian training must reach out to the disadvantaged in Christian love.

Notes

1. Based on Frank Riessman's observations in *The Culturally Deprived Child* (Harper & Row, 1962) found in Robert F. Biehler, *Psychology Applied to Teaching* (Houghton Mifflin Co., 1974), 460.

2. Biehler, 480-481.

The following resources may be helpful in teaching/learning through mission activities.

Barrett, David and Johnson, Todd. *Our Globe and How to Reach It.* Woman's Missionary Union, 1990.

Gallagher, Neil. *Don't Go Overseas Until You've Read This Book.* Bethany Press, 1977.

Schlabach, Gerald W. *And Who Is My Neighbor?: Poverty, Privilege and the Gospel of Christ.* Scottsdale: Herald Press, 1990.

Reaching And Teaching Through Vacation Bible School. Convention Press, 1984.

12. | Committees

Establishing Importance

When two or more are gathered in a local church, what do you have? A committee. One of the best examples of group work is the committee, whether it functions or not. Numerous jokes exist about the work of committees in a church. Often committees have received poor comments and evaluations. In fact, some churches are accused of having too many committees and being "committeed" to death. However, there is a biblical precedent for the effective use of committees.

After having led the children of Israel out of Egyptian captivity, Moses had the monumental task of managing their daily needs. From morning to night, Moses was involved in a variety of decisions. Soon the task became too great for Moses. His father-in-law, Jethro, advised Moses to delegate various levels of responsibility and to spend time instructing the people. Moses began to follow this pattern (Ex. 18:13-27).

The pattern established had two distinct advantages. First, the new pattern allowed Moses to concentrate upon the more crucial tasks. Rather than being bothered with every minute detail, Moses could concentrate on the issues that only he could handle. Second, the new pattern allowed for the development of leadership among the lay-persons of the Hebrew community. These individuals were learning how to be effective leaders by on-the-job training. The people worked together in a planned growth experience that benefited the entire community.

Later in Hebrew history, various levels of priesthood developed. Each level of priests had specific responsibilities. These responsibilities were shared in such a way as to make the task easier and more manageable. They worked together on tasks from administering religious legislation to working on the construction of the temple. Israel, the Chosen People, was to be a community of faith—a people working together as priests and prophets to the world.

In the New Testament Jesus had various levels of followers, from the great masses who followed Him to the twelve disciples. Behind the disciples were the inner three—Peter, James, and John. Jesus instructed His followers and gave them authority for the work He commanded. Forming groups of two, these individuals carried out the work of the Lord.

Jesus's last instructions were that His followers should go into all the world, teaching, preaching, and proclaiming the gospel. As this message was spread, churches—groups of believers—formed. As various tasks and needs emerged within the churches, groups of people were assigned the responsibility of meeting those needs.

In Acts 6, a problem arose concerning the care of Greek and Jewish widows. A group of servant/leaders, later called deacons, was organized to serve and meet specific needs. Among these early deacons was Stephen, the first martyr of the Christian faith. The apostles and others were free to do other parts of God's work. The early missionary journeys were conducted often by two or more people cooperatively working to proclaim the gospel. Accounts both in the Old and New Testaments give evidence of people working together to accomplish God's purpose. The work done today through committees has a biblical foundation and precedent.

Defining Chapter Goals

At the conclusion of this chapter, the learner should be able to do the following:
- state the biblical precedents for the work of committees;
- summarize seven key ideas regarding the nature of committee work;
- discuss ways that committees can improve their instructional function; and
- identify resources for committee work.

An Understanding of Committees

When properly understood, the nature and function of committees can greatly enhance their effectiveness within the local church. Without a solid understanding of its purpose, the work of the committee can quickly become misunderstood and distorted. Such distortion may lead to various levels of ineffectiveness; however, keeping its purpose in mind can greatly enhance its fruitfulness for the work of God's kingdom.

1. *Committees exist to do the work or enhance the work of the church.* If there is no genuine need or work, the committee should not exist. A committee is a tool through which committed Christians can be led by the Holy Spirit to do the work of the church. The committee is a means; not the end in itself.

2. *Committees are formed from the basic nature and intent of the church.* Each church must clearly define for itself what its mission is. What does the church seek to accomplish among its own members and among those nonmembers both locally and otherwise? Once the church has defined its basic mission, the church must outline its basic tasks in order to accomplish its mission. Basic tasks may include to educate, witness, worship, and minister. Once these tasks have been defined, the church must then seek the best possible structure for the accomplishment of these tasks. Often a committee will be formed to meet one or more of these basic tasks. The work of each committee must be centrally related to the overall work of the church. People working together through committees contribute to the work of the church.

3. *No one committee should have greater prestige than other committees.* Often various committees have gained the reputation of being the most prestigious, the most powerful, or the most influential in a local church. Such committees may be the personnel committee, the finance committee, the nominating committee, or the committee on committees.

However, each committee has the assigned responsibility of doing its part for the accomplishment of the work of the church. The mother of James and John requested that her sons be allowed to sit on the right and left side of Jesus. These were places of prominence. Jesus responded that these places of honor were to be given by the Father. In addition, Jesus taught that the first should be last and the last should be first. To be great is to be a servant of all.

Often committees may fall into that same mindset as that of those who ask to be great. Each committee is a part of a greater whole. In the Christian community, no one committee should have more prominence than any other committee. One work or function is no better than another. Paul wrote, "The eye cannot say to the hand, 'I have no need of you'" (1 Cor. 12:21). People need each other; committees need each other. Without one another, the work of God is hindered.

4. *Committees should be made up of individuals with the talents, interests, and commitments necessary for the functioning of that committee.* Every individual should not be a part of every committee. Committees have differing tasks, just as individuals have differing personalities and talents. Frustration can be avoided if there is the best possible match between the individual and the committee on which he serves. People work more effectively if they have the talent, interest, and commitment for the task.

5. *Not all work of the church should be done exclusively by committees.* Emergencies, needs, and opportunities emerge in which individual Christians must respond immediately. The committee is an avenue for corporate or group ministry. Certain tasks may be done more quickly and easily by individuals. Other tasks require the corporate working together of the church through committees. Care must be exercised in knowing the difference between the two. While we must work as individuals, we must nevertheless work together as a group. Both ministries, the individual and the corporate, are vital to a growing church.

6. *The committees are accountable to the church for their work.* No committee should become isolated. Each committee receives its assignment from the church; therefore, each committee is accountable to the church. In turn, the church is accountable to God for the accomplishment of its mission. Levels of mutual accountability must permeate the work of the church.

7. *Committees have a basic teaching ministry that is inherent within its assignment.* Through the committee experience, individual committee members receive training. Committees offer a wonderful experience in an intensive on-the-job training in Christian community. Lives are changed through committee work. Committees have a basic teaching responsibility for the individual and the church. This last distinctive will be the focus of the remainder of this chapter.

Teaching Role of Committees

In order for the committee to work effectively, there must be an overall instruction of both church member and committee member to the work of the various committees. How can they do the work unless they know how to do the work? How can the congregation make suggestions or offer assistance unless they know the proper ways of communicating? Various methods may be used to reach this goal.

1. *Explain and describe.* The work of the committee must be clearly explained to the congregation. Periodically examine how the committees function within the church to accomplish the mission of the church. This explanation should be made in a variety of ways. For example, the pastor in his sermon may address how each part of the committee process works toward the accomplishment of the mission of the church. Charts and diagrams may be used to show how the committees function. These may be printed in church papers and newsletters. This type of information should be done on an annual basis. This explanation will keep the information fresh in the minds of the members. Ideally new members are continually being brought into the congregation. New members need instruction; older members need reminding and reinforcement.

2. *Analyze gifts and interests.* Some type of interest or talent search is necessary. Such information will help identify the congregation's strengths and interests. Once these interests are known, people may be asked to serve in various ministry opportunities, including church committees. Observing the strengths and interests of members may help in identifying individuals and their particular place of ministry. Helping people find their service is a teaching ministry itself.

3. *Train and function.* Once committee members have been chosen, time must be spent in their training. It may be advisable to begin with the committee chairperson. Spend the time needed to train the chairperson on his job responsibilities. In turn, that person can devote the needed time to training individual committee members.

Place committee meetings on the church calendar. Two or more times during the year may be designated as "committee work days." During this time, all committees should meet and receive either an orientation to their assigned task or a "check-up" to determine the progress made toward their assignments. Making the committees meet at least twice a year will ensure that at least some level of instruction and accountability are present. Other meetings should be planned in light of need and nature of the committee.

Time must be given to studying the committee's job responsibility. In order to accomplish these tasks, the committee members must acquire those needed skills. List the skills needed to accomplish these tasks. If needed, special training sessions may be offered.

Next, help each committee to examine the current needs of the church, especially as it relates to its assigned tasks. Help them learn how to find pertinent information and identify significant needs. Stay informed with the work of other committees. If information is discovered, channel it to the proper committee. Try to avoid duplication of committee work.

Each committee should have some contact person with the church staff. In small churches, that contact person may be the pastor. In larger churches, various members of the staff may be assigned to various committees. These assigned staff members may then have the responsibility for training and keeping in contact with the committee.

4. *Report.* Committees should periodically report progress on their assigned task to the congregation. Such information keeps the congregation aware of needs and steps being taken to meet those needs. Reports from various committees help in keeping the congregation informed and aware that its committees do function. Reports should use the best possible ways of presenting the information to the congregation. Reports enhance the congregation's awareness of its mission, work, and opportunity.

5. *Evaluate.* Each committee should be evaluated to determine its effectiveness in doing its assignment. Strengths and weaknesses should be determined. Ways to improve effectiveness should be discovered and implemented. Some committees may need to be broken down into smaller committees. Some committees may need to be disbanded because of a lack of need. All members should be involved in the evaluation process. Evaluation itself is a teaching/learning experience.

Reviewing the Opportunity

Despite numerous jokes and caricatures about committees, committee work is still a valuable Christian growth opportunity. Committees allow for shared ministry and involvement for all members of Christ's community. The challenge is to go beyond the caricatures and to use committees effectively. Let the committee experience be a positive teaching and discipleship building one for both committee members and church members.

Notes

The following resources may be helpful in teaching/learning through committees.

Fransen, Paul. *Effective Church Councils: Leadership Styles & Decision Making in the Church.* Augsburg Fortress, 1985.

Haugen, Edmund B. *Mister/Madam Chairman: Parliamentary Procedure Explained.* Augsburg Fortress, 1963.

McCarty, C. Barry. *A Parliamentary Guide for Church Leaders.* Broadman, 1987.

Renton, Michael. *Getting Better Results from the Meetings You Run.* Research Press, 1980.

Sheffield, James. *Church Officer and Committee Guidebook.* Convention Press, 1976.

13. | Study Groups

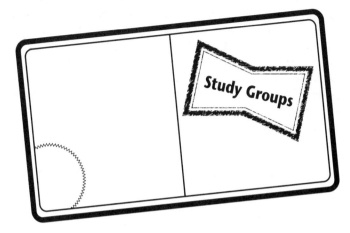

Establishing Importance

"Oh, no, not another group project," I responded after being handed the syllabus for a new seminary course. Working in groups had become a way of life in my seminary studies. My experiences had varied. On occasions the group worked together beautifully; on other occasions the group worked together horribly. Too often I felt I was the only one doing the work. Of course, others may have felt the same regarding themselves.

One brave soul in the class ventured forth a question, "Sir, why do we do so much with group work?"

The professor responded, "Most of the work that you will do in church involves groups of people. It is important to learn *now* how to work most effectively with them." He smiled and continued to describe our assignment.

Years have passed since that day. Most of the work done in churches, I have discovered, does involve groups. Like my seminary classroom experiences, my church work experiences have varied. Sometimes the group functioned well; other times it did not. Often I felt I was the only one getting things done. Other people may have felt the same about themselves. Indeed, a learning experience can match real-life experiences.

Group work is essential to the life and work of the church. There is no such animal as a lone Christian. Christianity involves a fellowship of believers working together—a group. Regardless of the quality of group work, it is an essential part of the process of discipleship.

Groups exist in churches for varied reasons. Fellowship and spiritual growth are two primary reasons for groups. Also, groups have a teaching/learning aspect which is the focus of this chapter. Following a general discussion of the nature of groups, leading a discussion group will be explored. The last section will deal with the book review, a technique often used in study groups.

Defining Chapter Goals

At the conclusion of this chapter, the learner should be able to do the following:

- identify two primary tasks of any group;
- describe the process of how groups develop;
- identify seven principles that enhance the teaching function of groups;
- identify seven ways of facilitating group discussion;
- list ways to improve the preparation and delivery of book reviews; and
- identify resources for groups and book reviews.

The Nature of Groups

Noted English poet John Donne wrote, "No man is an island." This observation is particularly applicable in describing the formation of groups. When two or more people join together, a new dynamic force is created. The new sum (the group) is greater than the sum of any of its parts (the individuals). As the parent of two children, I quickly came to realize the truth of that equation. Having the second child does not double the parental load, it triples or quadruples it, depending upon the nature of both parents and children.

Each group is different, possessing its own rules, standards, and codes of conduct. Like individuals, groups possess their own self-concept, or self-image or self-identity. Groups promote their perceived self image. For example, the young married class may view themselves as young, vital, creative, and unconventional. Often this group is hesitant to promote to an older class because of losing this image. If they joined another, older group, their self-image would be shattered. They would be old, dull, mundane, and conventional. The pastor's class (a Sunday School class taught by the pastor) may have the exalted image of those set apart for Bible study. It is a special privilege to be taught by the pastor. Often it is hard to be accepted as a new member of that class and even harder for an old member to leave the group. Groups develop images; in turn, these images direct the group.

Groups work at establishing and maintaining their identity by rewarding those who are faithful to the group's standards and by punishing those who violate the standards. Regardless of the individual's age, a tremendous amount of group pressure is exerted on his behavior and attitudes.

Each group has two primary tasks: the socio-emotional task and the instrumental task. The socio-emotional task refers to the emotional bonding and strengthening that must occur within the group to maintain its cohesiveness. It is the feeling of "we-ness" or "us-ness" in the group. Without this feeling the group will deteriorate, especially in Christian education where group participation is voluntary (unless it is required in a seminary class project).

The instrumental task is the one whereby the group fulfills its own basic task. This task is specified by the nature of the group. The task may be to study a particular book, to plan and conduct a church bazaar, to pray for one another, or to conduct a specific business of the church. The instrumental task is the reason for the group's existence.

Depending upon its nature, each group will vary in its emphasis on these two tasks. In Christian education, a balance must be achieved between the socioemotional task and the instrumental task. Some groups are very loving and yet accomplish very little, apart from fellowship. Other groups are not very loving and yet accomplish a great deal. Christian education must involve getting the job done and maintaining healthy relationships. Paul wrote that we should speak the truth in love. Speaking and doing the truth involves getting the job done, but in such a way that promotes the very reason for our existence. Paul wrote that without love, "I am a noisy gong or a clanging cymbal (1 Cor. 13:1)."

Groups are continually undergoing a process of growth and development. Such change is normal and healthy. Tuckman and Jensen have identified a model that involves five stages of group development.[1] The first is called *Forming*, which involves the group's seeking to identify its task, its rules, and its methodology. Do you remember being a member of a new group? How did you feel? Quite likely, you felt a degree of anxiety. Here anxiety is the norm. Individuals wait upon the leader to make the first move. Groups in this stage are highly dependent upon the leader. Often limits are tested to determine what is acceptable and what is not. This testing is like that of children trying to discover exactly how much they can get away with.

The second stage is called *Storming*, where individual members experience emotional resistance to the task. Here various expressions of rebellion occur. Members may display resentment toward the leader. They may ask, why should he be the leader, why not me? Individuals may disagree with whatever the group says in order to assert their own independence. The person may rebel by not participating, by showing up late, or belittling the opinion of others. Small coalitions may develop where two or more form a subgroup within the large group. The subgroup may compete and rebel against the large group. Often groups may disband at this point because of this early conflict.

If the early conflict can be weathered, the group enters the third stage called *Norming*, which reflects the resolution of these conflicts. Here cooperation is apparent as assigned tasks are attempted. People begin to do the business at hand, such as planning the retreat, itemizing the church budget, or engaging in intensive Bible study. A good feeling exists in the group as people cooperate and support each other.

The fourth stage, called *Performing*, involves the completing of the task. As group members accomplish the task, they disengage or remove themselves from the task and from each other during the fifth stage, *Adjourning*. Some groups are ongoing; their reason for existing is never completely fulfilled. Other groups exist for a specialized task; once the task is complete the group dissolves. For the group to continue functioning, a new task or project must be introduced. In the new process, it is common for the group to experience over and over again the stages of group development.

Working in groups has powerful potentialities for the teaching/learning process. In groups, members can learn from each other through mutual participation. Each can be a teacher and a learner. Group interaction provides an opportunity to express feelings and insights. In turn, members can receive feedback from other group members. Dorwin Cartwright (1951) has identified principles that have specific application to didactic or teaching/learning groups.[2]

1. *Consistent values and objectives.* To increase effective teaching/learning, both teacher and learner (leader and group members) should feel they have similar values and objectives. If one member feels "at

odds" with the group, resistance or obstacles are created. These barriers hinder the group's teaching/learning goals. Emphasizing the group's common goals and characteristics is crucial. Don't dwell on the differences; dwell on the similarities. Each individual must feel some common link with leader and group. Work to find the common threads which will hold the group together, strengthen its fellowship, and accomplish its tasks.

2. *Satisfying individual member needs.* Groups that meet individual needs are more effective in both maintaining the group and exerting influence upon the group. Each need cannot be met each time the group meets. Discover the member's needs and try to satisfy those needs as much as possible. Enlist the help of the group in meeting the needs of each other as the teacher or leader cannot do it alone. Every person can help. Let responsibility belong to everyone.

The more satisfying the group experience, the more likely for future teaching/learning opportunities. This principle has a great deal of application to Christian education. If Christian education has the quality that meets individual needs, we will not need to "beg" people to attend. People will respond when their individual needs—hurts and yearnings—are being met.

3. *Group leader influence.* What happens to the group leader influences the group member. If the group leader is respected, those people who associate with him feel a part of that prestige. If the leader becomes involved in questionable behavior, the entire group experiences the impact of the event. The leader must be consistently aware of his influence.

The quality of the leader's life greatly impacts the accomplishment of the goals of the group. This may be part of the reason that Paul wrote that we should not too eagerly desire the office of teacher. Those who teach will be more closely judged. The influence of the individual is primary with the power to help or to hurt people.

4. *Consistent methodology.* Methods used in the group must be compatible with the accepted norms of the groups. For example, in a group accustomed to the democratic process, being a dictator is going to be neither popular nor productive. Groups that are accustomed to giving input must be allowed to do so. Getting to know the people in the group helps in selecting the best method. Using improper methodology can alienate members, decrease participation, and encourage dropouts.

5. *Convincing the group.* The group must be convinced of the need

and the urgency of its task. Time devoted early to the importance of the task is not wasted. Periodically the group must be reminded of what they are doing and its relationship to the task of the group. Being "sold on the group" helps the group function and attain its goals.

6. *Clarity of communication.* Good communication is essential to the functioning of a group. If it is not present, misunderstandings can easily occur. Communication takes time. Make sure what is said is understood, whether it's a procedure or expressed feelings. Take the time to ask for feedback. Look for clues to understanding—facial expression, body language, and heads nodding. Take time to ask for questions or clarifications. If communication is "foggy," so is the teaching/learning process.

7. *Strains or conflicts.* Both the teacher and learner should be aware that conflicts will occur as a group functions. This tension is normal and healthy. Where there is no strain, there is no growth. Recognize and work through strains as soon as possible. Conflicts not explored early may build up, causing greater damage at a later date.

Discussion Groups

One group common to Christian learning is the study or discussion group. Such groups encourage growth in the development of information, understanding, attitudes, and skills. Various factors influence the effectiveness and productivity of such groups including how large the group is, how information is exchanged, how members interact, how conflicts are resolved, how leadership is exerted, and how decisions and problems are solved. In order to facilitate quality teaching/learning, several key ideas are important.

1. *Initially establish the rules for discussion.* Early in the group's formation establish the rules that will guide the discussion. Determine rules early to avoid needless later conflict. The group should formulate its own basic rules such as the length of discussion, the rights of individuals to varying opinions, and the avoidance of vague and general statements. Rules established and followed facilitate teaching/learning opportunities by avoiding unnecessary conflict.

2. *Allow and encourage each individual an opportunity to participate.* In any group of which I have been a part, a few individuals have tried to dominate the discussion. A good rule is that no one has the right to speak twice unless each has had the opportunity to speak once. Don't force anyone to speak. However, give everyone the opportunity. Group effectiveness is improved when all participate.

3. *Avoid generalities.* Generalities are those broad statements that are difficult to pinpoint. One that I hear constantly is "Well, all the other teachers allow us to do this." Parents often hear the one, "All the other parents let them do it." I remember using those words with my parents in my attempt to have my own way.

Now as both a parent and teacher, I have learned the importance of breaking down a general statement into specifics. For example, I respond to my students, "Give me specific examples of what you mean." Discussion is more profitable if it is specific.

In freshman English, I quickly learned that my essay examinations were too general in nature. I made broad sweeping statements that sounded good but were unsubstantiated by specific examples. If we generalize, we must include the examples that form the basis of our generalization. If a group member makes general statements, ask them to be specific. Being specific helps in clarifying ideas for both the speaker and the listeners.

4. *Share feelings in a nonjudgmental manner.* How we feel is not a matter of right or wrong. Right or wrong develops in what we do with those feelings. Create an atmosphere where people feel free to share their feelings. Feelings can range from hurt and anger to joy and peace. It takes courage to share feelings, to become vulnerable. If we criticize people for sharing their feelings, they are likely to become embarrassed, defensive, and absent from the group. Can we genuinely blame them for this response?

If one member must share something that may "hurt" another member, he should focus on the specific behaviors and his feelings. Do not make judgments on the other person. If Mary continually interrupts Jane when Jane speaks, Jane feels annoyed. Jane may say to Mary, "I feel frustrated when I am constantly interrupted." Or Jane may say, "Mary, you're rude and insensitive." Which statement is more effective for both individuals? The former statement deals with specific behaviors and feelings, rather than an attack on Mary. Share feelings in ways that help, not hurt, the person and the situation.

5. *Request feedback.* Feedback is a vital part of our sharing of ideas. Give and expect feedback from others. Feedback helps us to correct our own ideas, to hear ourselves, and to know how accurately we are being heard. Phrases that encourage feedback include—Is that clear? Does that make sense? What do you think? Discussion should involve interactive feedback, not solitary and serial monologues.

6. *Make all members accountable for keeping the discussion on*

target. In any discussion, "rabbits" appear that will be chased. However, let each member of the group be responsible for keeping the discussion on target. Consider the time restraints. A few softly-spoken phrases such as "How interesting, let's get back to the main idea" or "That's an interesting point, if we have time we may return to it," may help redirect attention.

7. *Accept positions and personalities.* In Christian discussion, there is no excuse for belittling any individual for his views. Fruitful discussion occurs only when we demonstrate acceptance of all people and their ideas. Following Jesus's example will greatly help us. While He did not accept all behavior, he did offer acceptance to all people. Offering genuine acceptance contributes to growth and maturity.

Book Reviews

One method often used in sharing information in various study groups is the book review. Book reviews are wonderful opportunities to introduce a subject to a group, to help the group in increasing its understanding of a book and to present an evaluation of the work. Walking past a bakery is similar to listening to a book review. The reviewer provides us with the aroma of the work. We then decide if we wish to take it home and enjoy it. Book reviews do not take the place of reading the book. Smelling the pastry is not the same as eating it. While volumes have been written about writing effective book reviews, summarized information will now be shared.

Preparing and delivering a good book review is no easy task. It requires thorough preparation that first includes *reading the work.* Many times, we may be tempted to review a work when we have not read it entirely, only having skimmed the book. To take the time to review a book requires having read the book. To do less is to do an injustice to the book's author and to your audience. As you read the book, *take notes.* Write down the page numbers of significant quotes, interesting illustrations, and significant descriptions.

In preparing the book review, the beginner should *write down the entire script.* More experienced reviewers and speakers may be able to get by with an outline. However, it is so easy to forget something or someone. As my wife and I shop in our small community, we often meet students. We have a silent rule. If I do not introduce her immediately, it means that I cannot recall the person's name. My wife immediately introduces herself and requests his name. The student quickly gives his name. This strategy has saved me much embarrassment from my memory lapses. However, I cannot use this technique in giving a book review. I must write every detail down clearly. It's amazing what we can forget in a moment. Write down as much as you need.

Consider the time limitations. The book review may last twenty minutes or fifty minutes. Keep within the allotted time frame. Remember important messages can be conveyed with a limited number of words. Noted for his conciseness, Calvin Coolidge said, "I do not choose to run." That one sentence says it all. Mere length does not always reflect greatness.

The following basic outline may help in preparing the book review for delivery.

1. *Capture the audience's attention with a vivid illustration.* The first words spoken in an oral book review should secure the attention of the audience. Don't stumble over your words. Prepare your beginning and speak confidently and clearly. Failure to capture attention initially may mean never securing attention. Securing attention and maintaining attention go hand-in-hand.

Capturing attention may involve reading a section from the book that is particularly appealing. Create a mental image for the audience by recreating a dramatic scene from the book. Make absurd statements that you will clarify in the presentation. Begin with a basic question and use the presentation to answer that question. Use your imagination as you try to "hook" the listener. Use the techniques of the author that "hooked" you on the work.

2. *Develop the theme or purpose of the book.* Focus upon those key ideas that will prove or illustrate the theme of the book. The reviewer must clearly understand the purpose or theme of the work. A book may deal with the theme of relationships, friendships, greed, jealousy, power, or prayer. Ask yourself what the author is trying to do. Does the author accomplish the purpose?

Select a few key ideas in the book that are appropriate and significant for your audience. Show how these ideas are developed in the book. Keep the following ideas in mind.

Make personal applications.—Relate instances from the author's life and/or work that have relevance or interest to those hearing the review. Find out about the author's background through the book jacket. Your local library can help you locate needed author information. What experiences of the author contributed to this particular work?

Move from general to specific.—With any general statement you make, provide specific examples to substantiate it. If you say the work is well organized, provide examples of how it is well organized. If the book is spell-binding, show how it maintains your attention.

Analyze symbols and images.—Look for any symbolism that may occur in the work. Do certain images appear over and over in the work? What do the images represent? Relate this symbolism to the development of the theme.

Compare to other works.—Relate this work to other works with which the audience may be familiar. Compare and contrast the work to any others that the author has written. What makes this book special in comparison to other works? Look for its strengths and weaknesses.

Focus on questions raised.—What questions did you have as you first read the book? What answers did you discover? What new questions developed in reading the book? Share with the audience questions still unanswered. The use of questions may be an appropriate way to structure your book review.

Limit your key ideas.—Select what is important and deliverable. Better that your audience remember hearing several important points than to forget all the points.

Relate the book to its title.—What is the significance? Why did the author choose the title? Is there a better title? Why?

3. *Conclude the review in a thought-provoking manner.* End your presentation with the same preparation that you did with the beginning. Involved in the conclusion are such items as challenges the author may have provided; unanswered questions, final evaluations, and questions from the audience. You may want to conclude by summarizing the major points. Leave the audience with a significant quote from the work.

4. *Practice your delivery with audience relationships in mind.* When delivering an oral book review, have a complete script or good notes. Don't rely on being extemporaneous. That's not faith; that's lack of preparation. However, don't read your review. Know it; practice it. Be sure to bring a copy of the book with you to your review.

Speak slowly and distinctly. Remember you are there to communicate with the audience. Don't try to impress them with your vocabulary. Choose the words and the delivery in keeping with their understanding. Use pauses as you feel it appropriate with the audience. Learn to follow their heart beat and breathing rate. Let the audience know when you are quoting.

Work at relating to your audience. Don't be thrown if something unpredictable happens such as a child crying, or someone turning over a glass of iced tea. Work with the audience. Keep your composure. As the saying goes, "Don't ever let them see you sweat."

Know when its appropriate for the fat lady to sing. That means end the review when the review is over. Don't belabor the presentation. Read, prepare, and deliver as you would have it done unto you.

Reviewing the Opportunity

Study groups provide intensive opportunities for teaching and learning, not only in content but also in process. Christian growth occurs as individuals work together in group experiences. Groups must be designed and utilized in ways to enhance growth possibilities. One common method used by study groups is the book review. When properly used, book reviews can whet the appetite of learners for further study. Learning in groups is a basic part of living in the community of faith.

Notes

1. Bruce W. Tuckman and Mary A. Jensen, "Stages in Small Group Development Revisited." *Group and Organization Studies* 2, 419-427.

2. Dorwin Cartwright, "Achieving Change in People: Some Application of Group Dynamics Theory," *Human Relations*, 1951, 4, 381-392.

The following resources may be helpful in teaching/learning through various study groups.

Bouton, Clark & Garth, Russell Y., eds. *Learning in Groups.* Jossey-Bass, Inc., 1983.

Dillon, James T., ed. *Questioning & Discussion.* Ablex Publishing Corp, 1988.

Ford, Leroy. *Using The Panel in Teaching and Training. Using The Case Study In Teaching and Training. Using Problem Solving in Teaching and Training. Using the Lecture In Teaching and Training.* Broadman, 1970, 1969, 1971, 1968.

Oppenheimer, Evelyn. *Oral Book Reviewing to Stimulate Reading: A Practice Guide In Technique for Lecture & Broadcast.* Scarecrow Press, 1980.

14. | Music

Establishing Importance

What comes to your mind in moments of crises? When you need comfort, what immediately comes to your mind? When you are happy or joyful, what comes to your mind? Many times for me, the first thing I recall is a familiar hymn or other Christian music. When my father died, the hymn, "Rescue the Perishing" came immediately to mind. No longer concerned about the welfare of my father, I was concerned with those family members who had not yet made a profession of faith in Christ Jesus. In moments of decision, I often recall the words to "He Leadeth Me." Comfort is gained by remembering that He does lead me. Music has always been inspirational and comforting to me.

Music has played a vital part in mankind's development. Music is universal, expanding the boundaries of time and space and being known both in primitive and advanced cultures. In fact, music is one of the few social characteristics that appears to be worldwide. Music in primitive cultures seems to have had a specific purpose, not just for entertainment or artistic value. Often music and songs were associated with religious rituals, love songs, part of story telling, and preparing for war.

References in the Old Testament show the role of music. Jubal is the first musician mentioned in the Bible (Gen. 4:21). In Deuteronomy 31:19-22, God gave a song to Moses to teach to Israel. Music was a part of the everyday life of the Hebrews from their feasts, festivals, and marriage celebrations to temple worship. The Book of Psalms contains songs for worship. Music was a pattern of both worship and instruction found in the Old Testament.

In the New Testament, music also shares a role in worship and instruction. Mary sang a song upon learning of the child she was to bear (Luke 1:46-55). The angels sang at the birth of the Christ Child (Luke 2:8-14). At the last supper, Jesus and His disciples sang a song (Mark 14:26). Traditionally, it is believed their song was from the Psalms. In prison, Paul and Silas sang (Acts 16:25). Music played significant roles in times of both joy and sorrow.

As young children, we probably experienced songs being sung to us by loving parents. As the parent of a two year old, one of our bedtime rituals is the singing of a few songs. Every night, my son gets in my lap and says, "More songs." Songs are a source of comfort, joy, and peace to us. Music offers a special opportunity for teaching/learning in the Christian faith. Several of these options will be briefly explored as music can be a special avenue of Christian teaching/learning.

Defining Chapter Goals

At the conclusion of this chapter, the learner should be able to do the following:
- identify various ways music was used in the Old and New Testaments;
- discuss various values of music today for the Christian community;
- identify seven ways with examples of how to use music in teaching/learning experiences; and
- identify resources for using music.

Values of Music

1. *Teaching/Learning. Christian hymns offer a rich source of Christian teaching/learning.* The basics of the Christian faith can be taught and learned through music. The first hymn I remember is "Jesus Loves Me." The message of that song is one that applies to all ages and depicts God's great concern for us.

Hymns are often based upon Scripture or scriptural references. The texts may be literal quotes of Scripture such as "The Lord's My Shepherd" found in Psalm 23 and "How Firm A Foundation" in Isaiah 41:10 and 43:2 (often the KJV is used). Scriptures are often paraphrased in such songs as "While Shepherds Watched Their Flocks" (Luke 2:8-14). Biblical figures of speech may be contained in hymns such as the shepherd (John 10:1) in "Savior, Like a Shepherd Lead Us" or the rock (Isaiah 26:4) in "Rock of Ages."

When studied carefully, music teaches us theology or beliefs about God and His creation. Hymns provide a basis for verbalizing our deepest thoughts and feelings. Singing hymns is an active way for involvement in worship. Hymns help us relate to other Christians throughout the world and throughout time.

2. *Witness.* Music is a way of proclaiming the gospel. The witness of music is tri-directional. Music can be our means of witness to God as we proclaim His sovereignty and majesty through solos, congregational hymns, instrumental music, and choirs. Hymns are a praise directed toward God.

Music is often a way of witness for ourselves. As we sing and listen to music, we may "hear" the voice of God. God may speak to us through music, providing comfort, guidance, and instruction.

Music is often a way of witness for others. Music is a way of opening both the hearts of persons and the doors of opportunity. Music can be a verbal witness to the grace and power of God. Music can provide the instructions needed to lead a person to the presence of God. Often doors for direct evangelism are limited; however, music is often a tool for proclaiming the gospel. Often choirs and soloists are given opportunities that other ministers may not receive.

3. *Inspiration.* Music provides an opportunity to inspire us to more positive Christian living and decision making. Music can be uplifting for those who are depressed. In moments of despair, music can minister. Music can be the gentle nudge used by the Holy Spirit to compel us to strive once again for the kingdom of God.

4. *Directional.* Music is one way of focusing our thoughts, our feelings, and our attitudes toward God and godlike concerns. By taking us away from the business of everyday living, music can lead us to higher ground. Music can point us to God's kingdom and our role in the kingdom.

5. *Community Building.* Through our active participation, music can build and strengthen relationships with fellow believers. In fact, music

promotes Christian fellowship. Our minds and hearts are often directed toward unity through music. Music not only builds fellowship with the present but also the past and the future. Music can link us with generations past and the generations to come. Music is a way of retelling the Christian story for the future.

6. *Worship.* Music has value in worship. As part of our being created in the image of God, we have a need to worship the Creator. Music is a significant way of worship. In Nehemiah 12:27-46 and Isaiah 42:10-12, music is portrayed as a way of worship.

In the New Testament, personal and congregational singing was emphasized as found in Matthew 26:30 and Mark 14:26. Paul wrote: "Let the word of Christ dwell in you richly; teach and admonish one another in all wisdom; and with gratitude in your hearts sing psalms, hymns, and spiritual songs to God" (Col. 3:16) and "as you sing psalms and hymns and spiritual songs among yourselves, singing and making melody to the Lord in your hearts (Eph. 5:19)." James 5:13 states "Are any among you suffering? They should pray. Are any cheerful? They should sing songs of praise." In Revelation, the redeemed of the Lord sing (Rev. 5:9; 14:3; and 15:3).

Music became a part of the growing Christian church. During the Reformation, John Calvin, leader of the Reformed Tradition, emphasized the use of the Psalms as worship. Martin Luther emphasized the use of hymns which often deal with aspects of the Christian life. Later, Watts and Wesley focused on gospel songs which emphasized testimony and outreach. Music has long been a part of the worship experiences of churches.[1]

Today music is still a vital part of the church's experience. Prior to the 1960s, church music was generally thought to possess two important characteristics: being both good (highest quality) and sacred (no secular connotation). Church music was often thought of as a language set aside, different from that of the everyday worshiper. Beginning in the 1960s, popular music gradually became a part of church music in various denominations. Today music in church has the same range and variety as the variety of those sitting in the pews.[2]

Ways of Using Music in Teaching/Learning

1. *Creating learning readiness.* Music is a great way to set the teaching/learning atmosphere. Music can prepare the learner for the lesson at hand. For example, if the lesson is on missions, you might

have someone play "Wherever He Leads, I'll Go." Or you might play a taped recording of "People to People." Both music and lyrics direct the person to various aspects of mission.

Music used in a variety of ways can direct the learner's attention away from the everyday problems and distractions to the teaching/learning purpose. Keep the music short and to the point, focusing and directing attention. Then concentrate on the lesson.

2. *Illuminating or directing thoughts.* Music can be used to direct thoughts toward specific issues or questions. As a background for concentration, you may present a picture or pose a question for the learners to consider. While they are considering the picture or question, play background music.

3. *Combining with other media.* Music can be used in combination with other ways of teaching/learning. Use music to supplement the other activities. Music can be combined with such items as drama discussion and art to enhance the teaching/learning.

4. *Understanding background information.* Background information can be used to enhance the teaching aspects of the music. Explain the who, what, when, where, and why behind music. Share with the group something of the life of the composer. Fannie Crosby wrote great hymns of the faith, such as "Blessed Assurance, Jesus Is Mine." Knowing that Fannie Crosby was blind enhances the commitment expressed in her composition. Relate the songs to the periods in the author's life. For Example, Bill and Gloria Gaither wrote "God Sent His Son" during a period of despair. They questioned how they could bring a child into a world of such turmoil. Both a child and a song were born.

Explain the Scriptural references used in the song. Describe the meaning of the images used. For example, in the hymn "Come Thy Fount" explain that an Ebenezar is a place or a monument to the work of God. We learn when we become acquainted with the texts upon which music is based.

5. *Personalizing of music.* Explain what the music means to you personally. Use it as a time of testimony to show what periods of time in your life this music was particularly meaningful. Involve the congregation in activities that call for them naming their favorite hymns and the reasons for the selection. Encourage people to create their own songs, learn to play an instrument, and to be involved in group singing. The greater the degree of personalization, the greater the effectiveness.

6. *Complementing theme and the church year.* Seek to match the

music and the theme found in the church year such as Easter or Christmas. Music should also complement the basic message in the worship service or the aim of the teaching. Consult the topic index found in hymnals to help in selecting the best music. Music can then reinforce what is being taught.

7. *Involving active participation.* Music is an experience that should be activity oriented. In worship services, the music through congregational singing is one way to actively involve the participants. Try to make the experience as meaningful as possible because for this moment all are participating. Music may be one of the few experiences in which children may participate in the worship services.

Vary the ways of participation. Have men sing one stanza and women the other. Have one side of the church sing followed by the other side of the church. Have someone sign one stanza of the song while everyone listens. Have people close their eyes and sing. Use various ways to enhance participation.

Reviewing the Opportunity

Music can keep us focusing upon biblical truths and focusing reinforces learning. Deep within ourselves we carry songs that we have heard. Over time, these songs become a part of who we are as people. Let the songs we hear, learn, and remember be ones of encouragement to us and others and ones of mature praise to the Creator. Use music opportunities to enhance both personal and corporate Christian growth and learning.

Notes

1. Vic Delamont. *The Ministry of Music in the Church.* (Chicago: Moody Press, 1980), 14.

2. Robert H. Mitchell. *Ministry and Music.* (Philadelphia: Westminster Press, 1978), 127-133.

The following resources may be helpful in teaching/learning through music.

Burroughs, Bob. *An ABC Primer for Church.* Broadman, 1990.

Etherington, Charles L. *Protestant Worship Music: Its History & Practice.* Greenwood Publishing, Inc., 1978.

Hooper, William. *Ministry and Musicians.* Broadman, 1986.

Hunt, T.W. *Music In Missions: Discipling Through Music.* Broadman, 1987.

Johansson, Calvin. *Music & Ministry: A Biblical Counterpoint.* Hendrickson Pub. Inc., 1984.

Lovelace, Austin and Rice, William C. *Music & Worship in the Church*. Abingdon, 1976.

Mitchell, Robert. *Ministry & Music*. Westminster/John Knox, 1978.

Osbeck, Kenneth W. *101 Hymn Stories* and *101 More Hymn Stories*. Kregel Publishers, 1982, 1985.

Smith, Judy. *Teaching With Music Through The Church Year*. Abingdon, 1979.

15. | Writing

Establishing Importance

One of the greatest tools for teaching is writing. This observation is especially true in the field of Christian teaching/learning. The Bible is the written record of God's revelation. We come to know God through the testimony of the Word. Writing allows for a broader audience than traditional teaching. In addition, writing can cross cultures, as well as history. For example, the Bible speaks to all cultures and all times. Like teaching, writing is not limited to a select few. Numbers of individuals have the ability to communicate effectively through writing. Good writing can be learned.

Numerous books and articles deal with effective writing. Writing for Christian publications has become an ever-growing endeavor. The types of writings desired by Christian publications are numerous and include devotional material, fiction, both short story and novel, articles, and poetry. Also many denominations look for writers of many kinds. While it is not possible to go into any great length in discussing writing, a few guidelines and resources will be shared that apply to all such writings.

Defining Chapter Goals

At the conclusion of this chapter, the learner should be able to do the following:
- identify five guidelines for writing;
- identify different types of writing where a Christian testimony is possible;
- identify sources to improve writing skills; and
- name selected workshops and conferences for Christian writers.

General Guidelines in Writing

1. *Keep the audience in mind.* Just as you teach, you must keep the audience in mind. Remember you are writing to communicate, not to mystify. Let your writing be such that effectively communicates with your intended audience. Writing styles differ depending upon the needs, interests, and educational levels of your readers. Keep the reading level of your audience in mind.

2. *Know what you wish to say.* Having a message to communicate is foremost in the writing process. Be sure that you have something that is worth sharing. Any number of possible topics exist. Focus upon what you know, not what you don't know. Write from your strength of knowledge and experience. Where needed, do the necessary research. Well researched material can supplement your current knowledge of the subject.

3. *Determine the best way to say it.* How you say it carries a great deal of importance, just as what you say is important. The following ideas may help in effective communication.

Illustrate broad and general statements.—If you make a statement about various ways of improving communication between marital partners, describe some of those ways. Move from the broad statement to the specific with numerous examples. Blanket statements will not help the reader; specific statements will help.

Create readable paragraphs.—Paragraphs should revolve around a central idea. The first sentence, the topic sentence, should give the major focus of the paragraph. The rest of the paragraph should develop the ideas set forth in the topic sentence. Often the last sentence summarizes the main ideas in the paragraph.

Paragraphs are manageable units for both the writer, as well as the reader. Do not make the mistake of having a single paragraph that goes on for several pages. Generally such paragraphs are not readable. Write with conciseness; use short paragraphs to help achieve this end.

Use strong language.—Make the words in your writing strong, not weak. Generally use the active voice, rather than the passive voice. For example, it is better to write: "Agnes asked the question," rather than "A question was asked." Avoid sentences beginning with "there is." Rework sentences, using strong language.

Use transitions.—Transitions are the connections between ideas in sentences or between ideas in paragraphs. Transitional devices include using a pronoun to refer to a person or idea previously mentioned in a paragraph; referring directly to a preceding idea in the same words but preferably in different words; repeating a key word from the preceding paragraph; and the use of transitional expressions, such as accordingly, a result, consequently, finally, for example, furthermore, in fact, likewise, otherwise, therefore, and similarly. Transitions clarify and connect.

Vary sentence patterns.—Varying the way you begin sentence patterns will alleviate monotony. Variations to begin sentences include an adverb; adverb and verb; prepositional phrase; participle phrase; infinitive phrase; noun clause as an object of a verb; and an adverb and a predicate adjective. Try for rhythm in writing, using some long and some short sentences.

4. *Rewrite the material.* The key ingredient in the writing process is rewriting. However, rewriting is often neglected. Never allow the first draft of work to be the only draft. Rewriting is reshaping and refining your work of art. Rewriting is an opportunity to improve the communication between you and the reader.

In rewriting, check for the following items: a clearly stated purpose; good organization; good expressions; and good mechanics including spelling and punctuation.

5. *Submit the material.* An important part of the writing process is submitting the material written. Regardless of how wonderful the written material is, it cannot become published without being submitted. Material stored in a filing cabinet or sitting on the typewriter will not find its way to being published by itself. If you would have your work published, you must submit it.

As previously described, you must consider your audience as you write. Considering your audience includes the type of publication to which you will submit. You need to know the kinds of articles a magazine desires. The place of publication must match the focus of your writing. Good writing often goes unpublished because it is not properly matched to the right publication. Most magazines identify the editor to whom you can submit your article.

Types of Material Needed

Devotional writing.—Devotional writing is an attempt to share with the reader some inspirational message. Generally the message is relatively short. Devotionals tend to have one topic or theme that is developed. Reading a devotional piece should allow the reader to draw his own inferences. You do not have to tell him; rather, show him through your word choice and illustrations what you wish to convey. Allow the reader to draw his own conclusions.

Feature articles.—The purpose of feature articles is to present information in an entertaining fashion. These articles often center around the idea of "how to"; personal experiences; and interesting people, events and places.

Short stories.—Short stories are a type of fiction which can be read in usually one sitting. The short story contains many of the same qualities of the novel, only on a small scale. The short story has characters, plot, and development. Christian publishers are in the market for quality short stories and novels with a Christian message.

Novels.—Novels are longer fictional stories, providing an opportunity to present important problems, to entertain, to challenge, and to inform readers. The length of the novel varies with most novels going beyond 60,000 words. While the novel is a work of fiction, it nevertheless combines real-life experience with imagination. It is a narrative—telling a story. It is best to write a letter to a book publisher before sending a manuscript.

Church newspapers and newsletters.—These are sources for the beginning writer. These publications provide an opportunity to begin to express oneself with a growing number of people. Write articles about the mission trip or the revival services. Share a special poem about God's love. Church newspapers and newsletters can be the starting point of getting into print.

Letters and other correspondence.—An important ministry, and yet one overlooked, is letter writing. We live in an age where people are less apt to communicate through letters. Instead, we use the telephone. Letter writing is a dying art; however, it is an important one.

Receiving a letter can be comforting to those who are ill and encouraging to those experiencing difficulty. Receiving a letter is especially meaningful. My freshman year of college was a particular difficult one with my father critically ill. One lady at church wrote me a brief note each week on pink stationery. Her "pink letters" went a long way to cheering up my week. Paul's ministry involved writing letters to the growing New Testament churches. Letter writing can be a marvelous way to teach others of God's love and power.

Reviewing the Opportunity

Writing is another avenue of extending a Christian witness through teaching and learning. The types of writing opportunities vary from leisure reading to scholarly material. Regardless of the type, a Christian message can be given through writing. Like any other worthwhile activity, good writing requires discipline. Many Christians have found a fruitful and fulfilling ministry through writing with its necessary self-discipline and expanding audience. Whether it be an article in an encyclopedia or a note to a friend, write so that others might believe and be strengthened in their belief.

Notes

The following resources may be helpful in teaching/learning through writing.

Burack, Sylvia K., ed. *The Writer's Handbook*. Boston: The Writer, Inc., 1991.

Dickson, Frank A. and Smythe, Sandra, eds. *The Writer's Digest Handbook of Short Story Writing*. Cincinnati: Writer's Digest, 1981.

Hensley, Dennis E. and Adkins, Rose A. *Writing For Religious and Other Specialty Markets*. Broadman, 1987.

Knight, George W. *How to Publish A Church Newsletter*. Broadman, 1989.

Ricks, Chip and Marsh, Marilyn. *How To Write For Christian Magazines*. Broadman, 1985.

Zinsser, William. *On Writing Well: An Informal Guide to Writing Nonfiction*, 4th ed. New York: Harper & Row, 1990.

National writing conferences include

Annual Christian Writers Institute Conference and Workshops—Wheaton College, Wheaton, Illinois. Write to Director, Christian Writers Institute Conference and Workshop, 388 E. Gundersen Dr., Wheaton, Illinois 60188.

Decision Magazine's School of Christian Writing—Roseville, Minnesota. Write to Director, *Decision* Magazine's School of Christian Writing, Box 779, Minneapolis MN 55440.

Seattle Pacific Christian Writer's Conference—Seattle, Washington. Write to Director, Christian Writer's Conference, Humanities Department, Seattle Pacific University, Seattle, Washington 98119.

Writer's Workshop. Church Program Training Center. Baptist Sunday School Board, Nashville, Tennessee. Write to Director, Writer's Workshop, Church Program Training Center, Baptist Sunday School Board, 127 Ninth Avenue North, Nashville, TN 37234.

16. | Conclusion

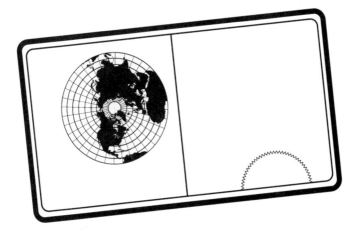

No doubt you are now thoroughly familiar with my concept of the teaching/learning process. This book is filled with the term and the concept. The work is built upon the concept of a passport which provides the basic credentials that allow for the exploration of new people, new places, new situations, and new teaching/learning. Obtaining a passport is only the beginning of an adventure. Likewise, this book is only a starting point for you as you explore the world of teaching/learning.

Part I focuses upon the foundations for Christian teaching/learning, including a biblical view, a theory of learning, the place of the learner, the role of the teacher, the lesson-planning process, and motivation and methodology. Essentially, part I is the *who, what, why,* and *how* of teaching. Part I provides the necessary elements in a passport to teaching/learning opportunities. Once the passport is secured, Part II deals with the various opportunities for teaching/learning.

Part II is essentially the *where* and the *when* of teaching. Specific contexts of Christian teaching/learning are addressed. These include the Bible teaching program, the worship service, leadership training, missions education, study groups, committees, mission activities, music, and writing. Remember the *where* and the *when* are more numerous than any one volume could hold. Go and experience more of those opportunities. Take what you have learned from this book and practice it in the real world of teaching. Continue to grow in your personal learning and teaching experiences. Let teaching and learning be a part of your personal responsibility and stewardship.

Each chapter contains numerous activities and resources to enhance your understanding and application. While I have attempted to present quality material on the subject, I have also sought to model good teaching/learning for the reader through the book's format, such as establishing importance of the topic; defining chapter goals; looking back and reviewing the opportunity (review); and looking ahead (previewing upcoming material). You are the best judge of my level of success.

Teaching/learning are integral processes. Philosophically, we must direct our teaching in ways appropriate to facilitate learning. We work as though it all depends upon us and pray as though it all depends upon God. While it has been discussed that we cannot really teach without learning occurring, this idea must be clarified. Each learner is an individual with his own choices. While I must work hard at my teaching, the learner is also responsible for his own learning. As a teacher, you are responsible for how you learn to teach and how you practice your teaching. Do all that you can, but remember the learner has his own choices. Help him to make the best possible ones.

I enjoy learning. As I grew, I enjoyed even more "learning how to learn." Being a teacher was never a childhood dream. I could think of few fates worse than being a teacher. However, God changed those desires, and I entered into a teaching profession. Since becoming an educator, I have discovered that teaching is a life-giving process. Seeing the understanding in a student's face is rewarding. Watching someone walk across the stage at graduation is purposeful. Witnessing someone have a second chance at learning and finding God's purpose of life is reassuring. All of the hard work involved in good teaching is worthwhile.

While few may become professional teachers, all Christians are teachers or witnesses of what they have experienced. In fact, Christian teaching is a part of the everyday experience of a disciple. This is the reason for this book—to help you learn to be a better teaching/learning disciple. As a part of my own stewardship, I have sought to convey my understanding for your consideration.

Christian teaching/learning is an adventure in faith. Ask any teacher. Faith is needed in God, in your learner, and in yourself. Teaching is growing in your own understanding and helping others to grow in their understanding. Christian teaching/learning is life giving as you share the gospel.

As a high school student I first became acquainted with the *Canterbury Tales*. Reading its Prologue, I became acquainted with the cleric or university student preparing for the priesthood. I will remember Chaucer's description of the man, "gladly would he learn and gladly teach." May this idea be characteristic of you as you practice your own teaching/learning.